Chronological Bible Reading Guide

God's Word the Word of Light and Life

JANE BECKER WEATHERS

WESTBOW
PRESS®
A DIVISION OF THOMAS NELSON
& ZONDERVAN

WestBow Press books may be ordered through booksellers or by contacting:

WestBow Press
A Division of Thomas Nelson & Zondervan
1663 Liberty Drive
Bloomington, IN 47403
www.westbowpress.com
844-714-3454

ISBN: 978-1-6642-1236-7 (sc)
ISBN: 978-1-6642-1235-0 (e)

Print information available on the last page.

WestBow Press rev. date: 12/01/2020

CONTENTS

GOD'S WORD: LIGHT AND LIFE

"In the beginning was the Word, and the Word was with God, and the Word was God. He was with God in the beginning. All things were created through him, and apart from Him not one thing was created that had been created. Life was in Him, and that life was the light of men."

John (John 1:1-4)

"I am the light of the world. Anyone who follows me will never walk in the darkness, but will have the light of life."

Jesus (John 8:12)

"Lord, who will we go to? You have the words of eternal life."

Simon Peter (John 6:68)

"Your word is a lamp for my feet, a light on my path."

Anonymous (Psalm 119:105)

"The revelation of Your words brings light and gives understanding to the inexperienced."

Anonymous (Psalm 119:130)

PREFACE

Spending time with Jesus and reading His letter with a cup of coffee is my favorite early morning activity. Over the years, my passion for the entire word of God, and its importance in my life led me to study how scriptures correlate, and this work is a result.

After reading through the Bible from cover to cover several times, I decided in 2005 to read it with a commercially planned chronological Bible reading plan. The plan listed complete books at a time, and generally three chapters of the Bible per day. This varied from a few short Psalms to quite a few pages per day in other books. Other chronological reading plans had similar problems. Books like Jeremiah and Daniel are not chronological.

After reading through the Bible, supposedly in sequence, but only book by book, I decided to devise my own plan. It became evident that daily portions could be an average of ten to twelve minutes a day, and a normal reader could read through the Bible in a year's time.

Dr. J. Vernon McGee, in his Thru the Bible radio program said that prophetic books should be studied with historical books, and someone should thread the prophetic books into the history where they belong. This guide does that to the best of my ability.

Many Christians seem to believe the only pertinent scripture for today is in the New Testament, but God preserved the entire Bible for those who wish to discover the whole counsel of God. I agree with A. W. Tozer who said, "We must not select a few favorite passages to the exclusion of others."

The importance of spending time in God's word was expressed by C. H. Spurgeon, who said, "If you wish to know God, you must know His Word. If you wish to perceive His power, you must see how He works by His Word. If you wish to know His purpose before it comes to pass, you can only discover it by His Word."

I am grateful to my husband Ted, and son Jeremy, for the suggestions and technical help they provided. This guide has been a work in progress for fifteen years, and is subject to change as new insight appears. I accept responsibility for misconceptions on time dating, and for the choice of accompanying scriptural portions, especially in the book of Psalms.

Jane Weathers
October 2020

INTRODUCTION

This guide has been compiled to give the Bible reader, whether a novice, or a seasoned through-the-Bible reader, an opportunity to read chronologically, not book by book, but chapter by chapter. A read-through in one year is not important, since the reader may go at a personal rate. The purpose of this guide is to include the supporting literature of poetry, prophecy, and epistles, as near as possible to the historical narrative of the times.

Dates in the first few chapters of Genesis are extrapolated from Ussher in *The Scofield Reference Bible,* King James Version. Other dates are based on Jones' "Bible Time Line;" HCSB: *Holman Christian Standard Study Bible;* the NIV: *Life Application Bible: New International Version;* and my Bible student husband Ted in the book of Daniel.

God's word does not give enough information to be dogmatic about all elements of time, and Bible scholars have different views about the dates of events.

Overlap and frequent review take place especially in the Kings and Chronicles, which contain information of the kings of Judah and Israel who ruled simultaneously. Some chapters cover events that occurred over many years of time. The gospels also contain much overlap and review.

Many Psalms do not identify the author or event, but the goal in placement is to associate the main theme or elements of a Psalm with the events of the time.

Keeping a day's reading to full chapters rather than a few verses here and a few verses there (with other narratives all happening at the same time) means that a true chronology is not practical or possible!

My prayer is that this reading schedule will arouse a deep desire to pour over the whole counsel of God to know Him better. May it increase understanding and provide guidance, as well as bless by shining the light of Jesus to brighten your day.

WEEK 1 READINGS

Day 1
John 1:1-5
    In the beginning
Genesis 1-3
    Creation: c. 4000 BC

Genesis 1-2: Other scriptures referring to creation include: Isaiah 45:18; Proverbs 8:27-29; Colossians 1:15-17; Hebrews 11:3; Revelation 4:11.

Genesis 1-3: The complexity of our bodies, our DNA, and even the perfectly formed tiny creatures show scientific evidence of irreducible complexity. The biological system must be completely intact to function properly as affirmed by the Institute for Creation Research. Albert Einstein said that the order found in everything convinced him it was no accident; there had to be a supreme being. The late Dr. J. Vernon McGee believed that throughout the period of creation, there was no death, so there could not have been an evolutionary process. His view is that Lucifer (Satan) fell between chapters 2 and 3 of Genesis. Death was a consequence of disobedience in the Garden of Eden.

Day 2
Genesis 4-7
    Cain and Abel: 3875 BC
    The Flood: 2500 BC

Day 3
Genesis 8-11
    Tower of Babel: 2242 BC
    Birth of Abram: 2166 BC

Day 4
Job 1-5

Events in Job: c. 2100 BC

Job must have lived a good portion of his life before Abraham was born. After two families of ten children each, and the accumulation of 22,000 domestic animals, Job lived for 140 years. The life spans of people in Abraham's time were close to this latter range: Abraham, 175; Isaac, 180; Jacob, 147; Joseph, 110. Parallels to the story of Job appeared in Egyptian and Sumerian literature between 2280 and 1600 BC (HCSB).

Job 3: Verse 14 says he would be at rest with "kings and counselors of the earth, who rebuilt ruined cities for themselves." NIV puts it "built for themselves places now lying in ruins." Some scholars think the Hebrew word ruins comes from the word for pyramid (Mazar, Vol. 4).

Day 5
Job 6-10

Job 8-9: Papyrus (8:11) was a marsh plant used for writing, baskets, skiffs (9:25-26), mats, and containers. The skiffs were boats used for fishing with nets. Many papyrus plants have now disappeared (Mazar, Vol. 4).

Day 6
Job 11-15

Day 7
Job 16-20

WEEK 2 READINGS

Day 1
Job 21-26

Job 26: Ancients, especially in Mesopotamia, believed the earth to be a flat disc floating on the water, and beyond the horizon were bottomless deeps and darkness. Even Job talked about it, and some of the prophets made similar comments. "He laid out the horizon on the surface of the waters at the boundary between light and darkness" (Job 26:10). "God is enthroned above the circle of the earth" (Isaiah 40:22). "I" (Wisdom) "was there when He established the heavens, when He laid out the horizon on the surface of the ocean" (Proverbs 8:27). A clay tablet copied in the 7th century BC shows the world as a circle surrounded by water (Mazar, Vol. 4).

Day 2
Job 27-31

Job 28: Glass was an article of luxury in the ancient East. Famous glassware was made in Tyre and Sidon, and Egyptians produced colored, not transparent glass, used in jewelry. Job said gold and glass could not compare to the value of wisdom (28:17) (Mazar, Vol. 4).

Day 3
Job 32-35

Day 4
Job 36-38

Job 37: Ancients thought the sky was like a flat roof, with the waters above. Elihu's weather report included the watery expanses and clouds saturated with moisture (vs. 9-12), and Elihu, who saw God as too far away to speak to us: "the Almighty—we cannot reach Him" (v. 23) asked, "can you help God spread out the skies as hard as a cast metal mirror?" (v. 18) Occasionally biblical references of rain were described as the windows of heaven being opened (Genesis 7:11; 8:2; Deuteronomy 28:12; Psalm 78:23; 148:4) (Mazar, Vol. 4).

Day 5
Job 39-42

Day 6
Genesis 12-15
> Abram entered Canaan: 2091 BC

Genesis 15: God's covenant with Abram was ratified by walking between the carcass halves (vs. 8-10, 17-18). A thousand years later God said of Abraham's descendants who disobeyed the covenant, "I will treat them like the calf they cut in two in order to pass between its pieces" (Jeremiah 34:18) (Myers, Kaiser).

Day 7
Genesis 16-18

Genesis 17-18: There was a difference in the laughter of Abraham and Sarah about the promise of a child. Abraham (17:17) may have seen God's promise as a hilarious miracle, but Sarah's laugh (18:12) may have been one of doubt and unbelief (McGee).

WEEK 3 READINGS

Day 1
Genesis 19-20
> Sodom, Gomorrah: 2085 BC

Genesis 19: Lot was involved in the government in wicked Sodom (v. 1).
The gateway was the official meeting place for business and government.
Lot despised the selfish lusts of his acquaintances. The open sin that he
saw daily became a normal scene that even his family seemed to accept.
Alexander Pope, an 18th century English poet, said in his Essay on Man V:

"Vice is a monster of so frightful mien,
As, to be hated, needs but to be seen;
Yet seen too oft, familiar with her face,
We first endure, then pity, then embrace."

Day 2
Genesis 21-23
> Birth of Isaac: 2066 BC
> See Appendix A

Day 3
Genesis 24-25
> Birth of Jacob, Esau: 2006 BC

Genesis 25: Jacob's "red stew" (vs. 29-30), also called "pottage" (v. 29 KJV),
may have spurred an old saying, selling something for a mess of pottage.

2000 BC is listed as the time Egyptians developed an alphabet of 24 signs, and built systems of irrigation from the Nile when it flooded (HCSB timeline).

Day 4
Genesis 26-27

Genesis 26: Gerar (v. 17) was on the edge of the desert where water was precious. To dig a well was to stake a claim to the land. To plug or stop a well was a serious crime and called an act of war. The Philistines saw Isaac's patience, and made a treaty with him (v. 28) to stop any future trouble (NIV).

Day 5
Genesis 28-30
    Jacob's ladder
    Birth of Joseph: 1915 BC

Day 6
Genesis 31-32
    Jacob wrestled with angel: c. 1903 BC

Genesis 31: Rachel taking her father's household gods (Teraphim) was a serious theft (vs. 19, 30-32). Jacob said the thief would not live. Laban could easily have replaced the idols, but according to official ancient archives, the Teraphim may have represented deeds or legal title to property, or they may have meant that the owner would inherit family leadership. Teraphims were also used by diviners. Tablets found southwest of Kirkuk, Iraq illustrated customs such as these from as far back as the patriarchs (Metzger; McGee).

Day 7
Genesis 33-35
    Isaac's death: 1886 BC

WEEK 4 READINGS

Day 1
Genesis 36-38
>   Joseph sold: 1898 BC
>   See Appendix B

Genesis 37: Midianites and Ishmaelites (vs. 25, 28) were distant relatives. Midian was the son of Abraham and Keturah (25:1-2). Ishmael was the son of Abraham and Sarah's maid, Hagar. Joseph's trip to Egypt may have been a 30 to 40-day journey, possibly chained and on foot (NIV).

Day 2
Genesis 39-41
>   Pharaoh's dreams: 1885 BC

Day 3
Genesis 42-44

Genesis 42-44: Judah was the brother who suggested selling Joseph to the Ishmaelites (37:26-27) and he probably lived with guilt for years as he saw his father's grief and remembered Joseph's pleadings (42:21). To save his father and youngest brother from more grief, Judah offered his life (44:33-34) as a slave, a sacrifice, and from him came Jesus Who offered His life as a sacrifice.

Day 4
Genesis 45-47
>   Jacob's move to Egypt: 1876 BC

Genesis 45: Joseph's words to his brothers (vs. 4-9) are an illustration of Romans 8:28, "all things work together for good...!"

Day 5
Genesis 48-50
>Jacob's death: 1859 BC
>Joseph's death: 1805 BC

Genesis 50: Shortly after Joseph's death, Hammerabi, king of Babylon from 1792 to 1750 BC developed 282 laws and rules with their consequences. His desire was to seek justice and prevent the oppression of the weak, even slaves. Included in the Code of Hammerabi was the familiar eye for an eye and tooth for a tooth law (History.com).

Day 6
Exodus 1-3
>Birth of Moses: 1526 BC
>Moses' flight to Midian: 1487 BC
>See Appendix C

Exodus 2: The strong faith and creativeness of Jochebed (Exodus 6:20) bypassed Pharaoh's harsh command. "We can envision her thought-life devoted to prayer. When we have no more resources and no more options at our disposal we lean into faith" (Macfarlan).

Day 7
Exodus 4-6
>Moses' return to Egypt

Exodus 5: Pharaoh, seen as Egyptian deity, said he didn't know anything about the Lord (v. 2). In ancient treaties the statement "Thus says the Lord, the God of Israel" (v. 1 ESV) was a demand from a superior ruler (Coover-Cox).

WEEK 5 READINGS

Day 1
Exodus 7-9

Exodus 7-12: The plagues in Egypt were "judgments against all the gods of Egypt" (12:12b). The Nile was sacred, as were the sun, air, and animals. These gods as brought forth in the plagues became offensive to the polytheistic Egyptians (Davis; McGee).

Day 2
Exodus 10-12
    The Passover: 1446 BC

Exodus 12: God saw the blood on the doorpost, and in His grace saw the Israelites as righteous and saved their lives. Each member needed to eat the lamb, but the blood on the doorpost was for the entire family (v. 23). God saved the little children that were too young to eat. The Passover portrays redemption as individual – each person must partake (believe), and those too young (under the age of accountability) will be saved at the end time (McGee).

Day 3
Exodus 13-15
    Crossing the Red Sea: 1446 BC

Exodus 15: God said if people obeyed God, they would not suffer from diseases like those of the Egyptians (v. 26). Later He gave dietary and cleanliness laws for their safety. McMillen in *None of These Diseases* describes how life habits can generate disease.

Day 4
Exodus 16-18
>Water from the Rock

Exodus 16:12-13: The natural time of quail migration from the Sudan in Africa to southern and western Europe is spring, with return in autumn. Large flocks of quail fly over northern Sinai and the Mediterranean Sea and are so exhausted that it is easy to catch them with nets or even bare hands. God may use natural events, but He is able to do this without migration (Mark 10:27) (Mazar, Vol. 1).

Day 5
Exodus 19-21
>The Ten Commandments given on Mt. Sinai

Day 6
Exodus 22-24

Exodus 23: God's caution that the worship of idols would be a snare to the Israelites (v. 33) was a warning of serious death consequences for idolatry. Pharaoh's officials who had seen death and destruction during the plagues, begged Pharaoh to let Moses and the Israelites go. They asked, "How long must this man be a snare to us?" (10:7) (Coover-Cox)

Day 7
Exodus 25-27
>Instructions for construction of the Tabernacle

WEEK 6 READINGS

Day 1
Exodus 28-29

Exodus 28: The wardrobe for priests emphasized holiness for reverential, not casual worship.

Day 2
Exodus 30-32
> Aaron's golden calf

Day 3
Exodus 33-34
Psalm 90
> A Psalm of Moses

Day 4
Exodus 35-37

Exodus 35: Offerings for the tabernacle (vs. 5-9) were transported during the wandering years. Before they left Egypt, the Israelites asked their neighbors for silver, gold and clothing. The Egyptians were favorable to them, and gave abundantly (12:36).

Day 5
Exodus 38-39

Exodus 38: Gifts for the tabernacle included mirrors (v. 9). A molten mirror found from the beginning of the eighteenth century BC had a beaten and polished reflecting bronze surface and a wooden handle with gold overlay.

The Holman Bible translated the contributions of gold and silver into pounds–over 2 tons of gold and almost 4 tons of silver. Many skilled men and women produced furniture, utensils, and embroidered curtains for the tabernacle (Mazar, Vol. 4).

Day 6
Exodus 40
>Tabernacle completed: 1445 BC
Leviticus 1-3
>Events in Leviticus: 1445 BC

Leviticus 1-3: The burnt offering in chapter one was voluntary to make payment for sins in general and is a picture of voluntarily coming to Christ. The grain offering in chapter two was also voluntary and was an offering of worship to show honor and respect to God. The fellowship offering in chapter three was voluntary, and expressed gratitude to God (NIV).

Day 7
Leviticus 4-6

Leviticus 4-5: The sin and guilt offerings in chapters 4 and 5 were required offerings. One life (animal) given, allowed another life (human) to be saved. Christ's death was the last sacrifice needed, and that human/divine life (the Lamb of God) provided for salvation. God "made the One who did not know sin to be sin for us, so that we might become the righteousness of God" (2 Corinthians 5:21).

Leviticus 6: The fire on the altar for the burnt offering was to be kept burning continually (v. 13) as a type of the access believers have to the throne of God any time of day or night.

WEEK 7 READINGS

Day 1
Leviticus 7-8

Leviticus 8: When a priest was anointed, blood from a ram was put on his ear lobe, thumb, and big toe as symbols to hear the voice of God, to use the hand for service, and to walk with God (McGee).

Day 2
Leviticus 9-11
> Nadab and Abihu's disobedience

Leviticus 11: Unclean animals might carry parasites and be susceptible to disease. In an early European plague, Jews enjoyed almost total immunity due to their dietary laws. The split hoof of a clean animal can indicate a separated walk with the Lord, and chewing the cud symbolizes meditating on God's word (McGee).

Day 3
Leviticus 12-13

Leviticus 13: Throughout Israelite history, laws were copied and recopied by scribes as legal and medical references for priests to give evaluations, advice and prescriptions. This was still the case in New Testament times when Jesus told the ten healed lepers to show themselves to the priest (Luke 17:14) (Mathews).

Day 4
Leviticus 14-15

Leviticus 14: Persons afflicted with skin diseases had to stay outside the camp (v. 3) until they were proclaimed healed and clean. It was outside the camp where the people dumped ashes (v. 12), buried corpses (10:4-5), sacrificed unlawfully (17:3,7), executed blasphemers (24:11,23), and where people with contagious skin diseases were banished. Jesus suffered outside the camp "so that He might sanctify the people by His own blood" (Hebrews 13:11-13) (Mathews; McGee).

Day 5
Leviticus 16-18

Leviticus 16: On the Day of Atonement with its sacrifice, a second goat was "presented alive before the Lord to be used for making atonement by sending it into the wilderness as a scapegoat" (v. 10 NIV). The sins of all the people were put on its head, and it was released to the desert (vs. 20-22). In like manner Jesus "bore our sins in His body on the tree" (1 Peter 2:24), "and the Lord has punished Him for the iniquity of us all" (Isaiah 53:6) (Mathews).

Day 6
Leviticus 19-21

Leviticus 20: An idol made after the Phoenician and Ammonite ruler, Molech (v. 2), was a brass monstrosity. Fire was made in the hollow center, and children were cast into the arms of the idol (Waltke; Smith).

Day 7
Leviticus 22-23

Leviticus 22: Acceptable sacrifices were to have no defects and be unblemished (v. 20). Jesus was the perfect sacrifice and salvation is through His death on the cross – He paid in full (Mathews).

WEEK 8 READINGS

Day 1
Leviticus 24-25
> Seventh year Sabbath
> Year of Jubilee

Leviticus 24: The light from the lamp stand in the tabernacle represented the presence of God. Jesus said, "I am the light of the world" (John 8:12). God's Word is light, and it is the word of God that brings people to salvation. The twelve loaves of bread were called "the bread of the Presence" (Exodus 25:30), and were a reminder of God's provision and presence every day. Jesus is the Bread of Life (John 6:32-35, 47-51), and He satisfies spiritual hunger (Mathews).

Day 2
Leviticus 26-27

Leviticus 27: People who had been dedicated to the Lord could be redeemed (vs. 2-3). Hannah promised to give Samuel to the Lord (1 Samuel 1:28), but if at any time she had wanted to bring him home she could have paid the established redemption price (HCSB).

Day 3
Numbers 1-2
> Events in Numbers: 1445-1407 BC

Numbers 1-2; Only men who could serve in the army were counted. Levites were counted in chapter three. Estimates range from 2.1 million to five million Israelites that left Egypt. Tribal camps carried standards (2:2) about five feet in length with an emblem at its top. The standards were: Judah – a lion, Reuben – a man, Ephraim – an ox, Dan – an eagle. Each of those tribes had two other tribes accompanying them carrying family banners (Mazar, Vol. 1; McGee).

Day 4
Numbers 3-4

Day 5
Numbers 5-6

Numbers 6: The Trinity is acknowledged in the blessing (vs. 24-26). God the Father keeps us. God the Son saves by His grace. God the Holy Spirit comforts and brings peace (McGee).

Day 6
Numbers 7

Day 7
Numbers 8-10

Numbers 10: The identification of Hobab (v. 29) varies in Bible translations, as does the name of Moses' father-in-law, Reuel (Exodus 2:18) or Jethro (Exodus 3:1). The terms father, grandfather, even brother-in-law are not consistent, so relationships are not always clear. Hobab's family lived in Canaan and most likely were nomads who knew the land, and where to find water. However, it was God who led with the cloud to the camping spots (Cole).

WEEK 9 READINGS

Day 1
Numbers 11-13
> The twelve spies: 1445 BC

Numbers 12: Moses was humble (v. 3), yet he was not afraid to face Pharaoh, the greatest monarch in the world; but Moses was angry when God was dishonored with idolatry. Jesus did not complain about words spoken against Him, but He was angry with those who spoke against God (MacArthur).

Numbers 13: The 40 days of exploration at 12 to 15 miles a day for 40 days (v. 25) would have been a 350 to 400 mile journey. This traveling time was reported in Egyptian military campaigns of Thutmose III in 1504-1456 BC, shortly before the spies explored the land (Cole).

Day 2
Numbers 14-15

Day 3
Numbers 16-17
> Korah's rebellion: 1426 BC

Numbers 16: As a Levite, Korah had a favored status among the Israelites in taking care of the holy tabernacle, but he wanted more prominence. Dathan and Abiram were from the tribe of Reuben, the firstborn of Jacob. Firstborns carried on the family's religious traditions, but Reuben had been set aside because of immorality. When God showed His choice of Levite leadership and punished the rebellious ones, the rest of the people were afraid they would also die. But "The next day the entire Israelite community complained" (v. 41) again, accusing Moses and Aaron. The repentant were saved by the very ones they had been against (v. 46). Jesus saves those who are against Him when they repent (Cole; McGee).

Day 4
Numbers 18-20
Water from the rock: 1407 BC

Numbers 20: Moses was only to speak to the rock for God's provision of water (v. 8). The grumbling, quarreling, and rebellion had discouraged the leaders, and Moses, as leader and model for the nation, dishonored God. His disobedience prevented this miracle from being a type of receiving access to God by speaking. Christ the Rock was struck (crucified) only once. Jesus gives the believer living water "springing up within him for eternal life" (John 4:14) (Cole; NIV).

Day 5
Numbers 21-22
Bronze serpent
Balaam

Day 6
Numbers 23-25

Numbers 25: Balaam worked for all kings and all gods. His counsel to Balak was to hurt from the inside (Revelation 2:14). After Balaam's visit, the Moabite women invited Israelites to their sacrifices to Baal, and immoral relationships took place (vs. 1-2). Balaam was slain in vengeance by the Israelites (Numbers 31:8, 15-16). Jesus was betrayed from the inside by one of His own, and condemned by His Jewish leaders (McGee; NIV; Jeremiah).

Day 7
Numbers 26-27

WEEK 10 READINGS

Day 1
Numbers 28-30

Numbers 28-29: All of the exacting details of the sacrificial system still excluded all by the high priest from meeting God in the most holy place (Leviticus 16:29-34). Because of Christ's sacrifice when the temple curtain of separation was torn, requests can be made directly to God through Jesus: "For there is one God and one mediator between God and humanity, Christ Jesus, Himself human" (I Timothy 2:5).

Day 2
Numbers 31-32

Day 3
Numbers 33-34

Numbers 33: The wilderness itinerary listed more than 40 moves in 40 years. The people transported a lot of belongings, and when asked, were able to give abundantly for the tabernacle (Exodus 25:1-7).

Day 4
Numbers 35-36
Deuteronomy 1
     Events in Deuteronomy: 1406 BC

Numbers 35: The tribe of Levi was not promised allotted land, but as ministers, they were given 48 cities throughout the land in which to live. Their presence among the twelve tribes was to provide a constant reminder of the need to be righteous and holy since all Israelites were the people of God. Levites were given means to provide for their families (vs. 2-3) in addition to what they received during sacrificial duties at the tabernacle (Joshua 14:4) (Cole; Merrill).

Deuteronomy means second law, and could be viewed as the constitution of Israel in Canaan. It was also a review of past historical events. Over and over God said to Moses, "teach them" (5:31). His messages in this book fulfilled that command to teach the law to the people camped by the Jordan River. It was here that he wrote the book of the Law (the books of the Pentateuch) (Deuteronomy 31:9, 24). At this time manna was still provided for the Israelites until after they entered the promised land (Joshua 5:12) (Merrill; Holdcroft).

Day 5
Deuteronomy 2-3

Deuteronomy 2-3: The destruction of Sihon and Og eliminated a hopelessly unrepentant people who would have corrupted the Israelites even before they crossed the Jordan (Merrill).

Day 6
Deuteronomy 4-5
The Ten Commandments

Day 7
Deuteronomy 6-8
The Shema

Deuteronomy 8: During the 40 years of Israelite wandering, the peoples' clothes and sandals did not wear out, and their feet didn't swell (v. 4). Eating the same diet over a long time period can cause beriberi, with swelling of the feet being one of the symptoms. Beriberi can also be caused by a thiamine deficiency, or by poor nourishment. The cardiovascular and nervous symptoms may be affected in this life-threatening disease. (healthgrades.com).

Week 11 Readings

Day 1
Deuteronomy 9-11

Deuteronomy 11: Moses wanted the Israelites to recognize how different life with God's blessings in Canaan would be from the hard life of slavery in Egypt (vs. 10-15). Egypt was famous for its irrigation system of canals from the Nile to produce lush gardens, but this required hard work from the Israelite slaves. A shaduf, as Arabs call it, was a beam balanced on a post with a bucket suspended from one end. A slave used hand or foot (v. 10) to lower the bucket into a pond at the end of a canal and swing it over to water the plant life. In the Promised Land rain would come at the right times for good crops if they loved and obeyed God (v. 13) (Mazar, Vol. 1).

Day 2
Deuteronomy 12-14

Deuteronomy 12: The Israelites were to worship at one place, in the place and time of God's choosing (vs. 11-14). Today God can be worshipped at any moment and place around the Person of the Lord Jesus in spirit and Truth (Tenney; NIV).

Day 3
Deuteronomy 15-17

Day 4
Deuteronomy 18-20

Deuteronomy 18: Moses prophesied about Jesus. He said God would raise up "a prophet like me…You must listen to him" (v. 15). What similarities are there? At times of birth both kings destroyed infant boys. The plagues in Egypt were miraculous, and Jesus performed many miracles. Miriam and Aaron doubted Moses' leadership (Numbers 12), and Jesus' family doubted Him (Mark 3:21). Moses put a serpent up on a pole to save lives, and Jesus mentioned this before He was hung on a cross to save lives (Missions Mosaic, 8/14) (see Appendix C).

Day 5
Deuteronomy 21-23

Day 6
Deuteronomy 24-27

Deuteronomy 24-25: Millstones (24:6) were similar to a mortar and pestle used by women to grind grain for their daily bread. The scales (25:13) may have been bronze, and iron ore weights were made in different shapes and sizes (Mazar, Vol. 1).

Day 7
Deuteronomy 28

Deuteronomy 28: The first fourteen verses abound with many blessings promised for obedience, but almost four times as much space is taken to tell about the devastating consequences of disobedience: the refusal to trust and obey.

WEEK 12 READINGS

Day 1
Deuteronomy 29-31
> Joshua given leadership

Deuteronomy 29-30: The covenant at Horeb (29:1) was the Ten Commandments. The Palestinian Covenant of chapters 29-30 says the land and the people go together. The promise of ownership of the land was unconditional, but possession of the land was conditional, based on obedience (McGee).

Day 2
Deuteronomy 32
Psalm 91
Deuteronomy 33

Psalm 91: Occasionally two adjacent Psalms were originally written as one Psalm. Although this is not noted for Psalms 90 (with Exodus 34) and 91, there are parallels between them and Moses' songs in Deuteronomy. The Rock is mentioned five times in Psalm 91, and the Lord is named as a firm, secure foundation, our salvation and protection, found multiple times in these chapters.

Day 3
Deuteronomy 34
> Moses' death: 1406 BC
Joshua 1-3
> Spies sent to Jericho: 1406 BC
Psalm 114

Deuteronomy 34: Moses could have been called a prince, a shepherd, a spokesperson, a miracle worker, a prophet or a national leader. Scripture bestows the highest privilege – calling him a servant of the Lord (v. 5) (Tilley).

Joshua 2: All nations had heard of the Lord God (v. 10), and how He delivered the Israelites. Only Rahab believed, acted on it, and was saved. The scarlet cord at Rahab's window typifies the blood on the doorposts at Passover. Both times the people in the house were saved from certain death (Exodus 12:13, Joshua 6:23) (NIV).

Day 4
Joshua 4-6
      Crossing the Jordan: 1406 BC
      The March around Jericho

Joshua 6: Archaeological expeditions of the ruins of Jericho by Dr. John Garstang (1929-36) showed that its walls did fall down flat. Two walls thirty feet high–the outer wall six feet thick, and an inner wall twelve feet thick–were joined by houses built on top (2:15). The outer wall dragged everything with it (Hess; Halley).

Day 5
Joshua 7-8

Day 6
Joshua 9-10
      God's victory with sun and hail

Day 7
Joshua 11-13
      Division of the land: c. 1385 BC

Joshua 11: The battles of chapters 1-12 took five to seven years to complete. It was because of hard hearts "that they would…be completely destroyed without mercy… just as the Lord had commanded Moses" (v. 20). God ordered the defeat of these nations to protect the Israelites from Canaan's corrupt influence, and to judge the hopelessly unrepentant people. Archaeologists expressed amazement that God did not destroy Canaan's cities sooner. Rahab and the Gibeonites believed and were physically saved (Joshua 6:25; 9:22-26) because they had heard and believed all that the Lord had done for Israel (Merrill; Coker; Hess).

Joshua 12: The list of 31 conquered kings is similar to how the pharaohs described their victories. Egyptian hieroglyphic writings show prisoners tied together with the name of a conquered town on each figure (Hess; Halley).

WEEK 13 READINGS

Day 1
Joshua 14-15

Day 2
Joshua 16-18
> Tent of meeting set up

Joshua 18: The scouts wrote legal documents (v. 9) used for land distribution. The lot was used to divide the land among the tribes (v. 10), and also for making decisions, settling disputes, assigning duties, and obtaining war spoils. Priests would seek God's guidance in prayer and consult the Urim and Thummim which were kept in a pouch on the priest's breastpiece. The casting of lots is not defined in the Bible. Some scholars think it could have been a couple of pebbles or precious stones in a pouch: one meant yes, and the other one meant no. The one pulled out of the pouch gave the answer. This put the decision making in God's, not man's hands. This method was still in use when soldiers cast lots for Jesus' garments at His crucifixion. (Hess; Hamilton; NIV).

Day 3
Joshua 19-21

Day 4
Joshua 22-24

Day 5
Judges 1-2
> Joshua's death: c. 1380 BC
Judges 17

Judges 1: God gave the victory when Bezek attacked, but then the Israelites adopted the godless king's method of punishment (v. 6) instead of following God's command to destroy everyone in the heathen nations (Deuteronomy 7:1-2).

Judges 17 to 21 must have preceded the times of the judges. The priest, Phinehas (Joshua 22:31, 33; Judges 20:28), was Aaron's grandson, born circa 1450 BC, and the Levite, Jonathan (18:3, 30), perhaps of similar age, was Moses' grandson (17:7; 18:30) (McGee).

Day 6
Judges 18-19

Judges 18-19: The Israelites did not follow through and capture all of their allotted territory. The tribe of Dan was given enough land (Joshua 19:40-48), but they failed to trust God to help them conquer the territory. They took two cities and then sent scouts looking for more land (18:2) because "the Amorites forced the Danites into the hill country, and did not allow them to go down into the valley" (1:34). Laish (18:27) was burned, rebuilt, and renamed Dan, or the Camp of Dan (13:25).

Day 7
Judges 20-21

Judges 20-21: The tragedy in chapter 19 brought unity to the tribes from Dan at the northern border to the southern town of Beersheba. A huge army from all the land almost annihilated the Benjamites who had protected the guilty. Remorse over losing a tribe of Israel caused them to help the remnant of 600 recover, find wives, and restart the tribe of Benjamin.

Week 14 Readings

Day 1
Judges 3-4
>   Beginning period of the judges (approximately 300 years)
>   Deborah and Barak: c. 1320 BC

1334 BC: Tutankhamon (King Tut), boy king at nine years of age, ruled in Egypt about this time for only ten years until his death in 1324 or 1323 BC. He married when he became king, and there is record of two daughters, which may have been stillborn. In 1922 archeologists Carter and Herbert discovered his artifacts in his tomb as preserved for 3000 years (Biography.com).

Day 2
Judges 5-6

Day 3
Judges 7-8
>   Gideon's 300: c. 1200 BC

Judges 7: Gideon's worship of God (v. 15) preceded this victory. "At the beginning of the middle watch" (v. 19) would have been at midnight, during the hours of deep sleep. In the dark, 300 pottery jars were smashed on the rocks, 300 torches that had been hidden inside the pitchers suddenly lit up the night with repeated blasts from 300 ram's horns and much shouting (vs. 19-21). One in a hundred soldiers might have a horn, so it sounded like 300 companies (30,000 troops) surrounded them. The 135,000 awakened Midianites panicked, and turned on each other before the Israelite army conquered them. This was not just psychological strategy–it was the Lord who gave the victory (Duguid; Ellicott, Vol. 2; McGee; Mazar, Vol. 2).

Day 4
Judges 9-10

Day 5
Judges 11-12
Jephthah: c. 1170 BC
Ruth 1

Judges 11: Jephthah's sacrifice of his daughter was not a slaying. God protected this family just as He did not let Abraham follow through with sacrificing Isaac. The translation for verse 31 should be: what comes out of the door of my house shall surely be the Lord's or I will offer a burnt offering. The sacrifice was that Jephthah's daughter would never marry. For a Hebrew woman this was worse than dying, but she honored her father's vow (v. 37) (McGee).

Day 6
Ruth 2-4
Ruth and Boaz: c. 1140 BC
Judges 13
Birth of Samson: c. 1120 BC

Day 7
1 Samuel 1-3
Birth of Samuel: c. 1105 BC

1 Samuel 3: The lamp in the tabernacle burned through the nighttime (Exodus 27:21). It is possible that Samuel tended the lamp as he was lying down in the tabernacle. "Before the lamp of God had gone out" (v. 3), suggests that God may have called Samuel just before dawn. Samuel would have been a teenager at this time (McGee).

Week 15 Readings

Day 1
Judges 14-16
> Samson's death: c. 1060 BC

Judges 14-16: Samson, a Nazarite from birth, violated every Nazarite vow during his lifetime, but he is listed in the heroes of faith in Hebrews. He did on occasion call out to the Lord for help, and as the angel told his mother, he began to deliver Israel from the power of the Philistines (13:5).

Day 2
1 Samuel 4-6
> Philistines' victory: c. 1055 BC

1 Samuel 4: There was no command to take the Ark of the Covenant out of the tabernacle at Shiloh, but the Israelites remembered Joshua's army carrying the ark around Jericho (Joshua 6:8). They thought it would give them victory at this time (v. 3), and Eli's two wicked sons brought the ark (v. 4). The Philistines knew of Israelite happenings, even from 400 years earlier, because they cried out, "Woe to us, who will rescue us from the hand of these magnificent gods...that slaughtered the Egyptians with all kinds of plagues?" (Beyer).

Day 3
1 Samuel 7-9
> Israel's demand for a king

Day 4
1 Samuel 10-12
    Saul's reign: 1050-1010 BC

Day 5
1 Samuel 13-14

1 Samuel 13: With no swords or spears (v. 22), soldiers may have used farm implements as well as bows and weapons of wood or stone. Farmers used the iron sickle and axe. The process of iron smelting had been developed between 1200 BC and this time of 1000 BC (Mazar, Vol. 2; Beyer).

Day 6
1 Samuel 15-16
Psalm 138
    See Appendix D

1 Samuel 15: Saul began his kingship with humility and trust in God, but he was impulsive and lacked discernment. "Turned away" (v. 11) describes a conscious decision to not follow the Lord. Samuel spent the night weeping, and did not initiate another visit (Beyer).

Day 7
1 Samuel 17
    David and Goliath
Psalms 14, 15

1 Samuel 17: David was already a warrior (16:18) when he was called into Saul's service as a harpist and armor-bearer (16:21). For David to try on the king's armor (17:38-39), he and Saul must have been similar in physique, and Saul was unusually tall (10:23). Immediately after killing Goliath, Saul sent David to battle, and with his successes, he was put in command of the soldiers (18:5), not a job for a teenager. Some others were referred to as youths when they were grown: Jeremiah protested when God called him, saying he was but a child (Jeremiah 1:6). Benjamin's brothers who hoped to save him from slavery called him "the boy" (Genesis 44:30), and not long after this, ten sons of Benjamin were named (Genesis 46:21).

Week 16 Readings

Day 1
1 Samuel 18
     Jonathan's love, Saul's jealousy
Psalms 133, 145
Psalms 103, 36

1 Samuel 18: "True friendship is a beautiful thing. A true friend listens, supports, comforts, guides, encourages, challenges, and loves the other. Pray for wisdom to be a true friend to those God brings into your life" (Macfarlan).

Day 2
1 Samuel 19
Psalms 143, 59
Psalms 12, 17

Day 3
1 Samuel 20
     Jonathan's archery message to David
Psalms 70, 86

Day 4
1 Samuel 21
     David's flight from Saul: c. 1015 BC
Psalms 6, 11, 28
Psalms 34, 56

Day 5
1 Samuel 22
Psalm 52
1 Samuel 23
>David saves Keilah
Psalm 25

1 Samuel 22: Nob, the city of priests and their families (v. 19) was near Gibeah, where the tabernacle was set up after Shiloh had been destroyed. Gibeah was also Saul's hometown and his capital (Payne).

Day 6
1 Samuel 24
>Saul's life spared
Psalms 57, 142,
Psalms 7, 35, 64

1 Samuel 24: David's character is clearly displayed in this chapter, and he followed God's way as expressed at a later time: "Bless those who persecute you; bless and do not curse" (Romans 12:14).

1 Samuel 24: To "cut off" (v. 21) one's dependents was the common practice in heathen nations. A new king would annihilate the previous king's family members who might want to capture the throne. An early example of this in Israel was when Gideon's son, Abimelech, murdered his brothers. It was then that the people of Shechem wanted to make him king (Judges 9:5-6). David had already promised his friend Jonathan that he would not destroy his family (1 Samuel 20:14-15, 42), and here he repeated his resolve to Saul. Then David went back into hiding (24:22).

Day 7
1 Samuel 25
>Samuel's death
Psalm 109

WEEK 17 READINGS

Day 1
1 Samuel 26
Psalm 54
1 Samuel 27
> David at Ziklag: 1012 BC
Psalms 140, 141

1 Samuel 27: Achish, King of Gath, granted David's request for refuge with the idea that the enemy of his enemy was his friend. David seemed to be his loyal servant according to his reports of military campaigns. These reports of fighting in Judah's territory were technically correct, though he was destroying future enemies and leaving no one alive to send back reports to the Philistine king (Beyer).

Day 2
1 Samuel 28-29
Psalms 22, 27, 58

Psalm 22: David was a fugitive due to Saul's fear and hatred, and even after Saul confessed that David was more righteous than he, and he would no longer fight him, David knew he was not safe in his own country. To David deep in distress, it may have seemed that God had forsaken him. God was "so far" away (vs. 1, 11, 19), and had rejected his cries for help (v. 2). Yet David told of past victories (vs. 4-5) and ended this inspired Messianic psalm with praises and determination to tell the next generation about the Lord.

Day 3
1 Samuel 30
Psalms 10, 124
1 Samuel 31
    Saul, Jonathan's deaths: 1010 BC
1 Chronicles 10

Day 4
2 Samuel 1-2
    David crowned at Hebron: 1010 BC
Psalm 2

Day 5
1 Chronicles 11
    David's reign: 1010-970 BC
Psalms 21, 110
1 Chronicles 12

1 Chronicles 12: David's early chief soldiers are named here. Overwhelming support of over 340,000 troops came from all of the tribes to make David king (vs. 23-38). The chapter ends, "Indeed, there was joy in Israel" (v. 40) (Beyer).

Day 6
2 Samuel 3
Psalms 40, 131
2 Samuel 4

Day 7
2 Samuel 5
1 Chronicles 13-14
Psalms 16, 108, 122

2 Samuel 5: The capture of Jerusalem and David's move from Hebron has been called the most important geographical move in the Bible, made possible when David found the water channel that Jebusites used in time of siege to bring water from the spring at Gihon, outside the city wall (v.

8). Scholars believe this to be the fifty-foot sloping tunnel shaft, with stair steps cut through solid rock, discovered in 1866 by British Army officer and archeologist Sir Charles Warren. A thick wall surrounded the city on the hill and this secret passage between city and spring was David's only way to gain entrance, which surprised the Jebusites. They should have been conquered earlier, but the Israelites had been unable or unwilling to attack (Mazar, Vol. 2; Beyer; Halley).

WEEK 18 READINGS

Day 1
2 Samuel 6
Psalm 68
1 Chronicles 15

1 Chronicles 15: For close to a hundred years the ark had been missing. It may have been David's joy in the Lord that Michal despised. Her interest in idolatry was noted when she used an idol as a dummy to resemble a sick husband (1 Samuel 19:13) (Beyer).

Day 2
1 Chronicles 16
Psalms 1, 19, 33
Psalms 75, 100

Day 3
2 Samuel 7
          Davidic covenant: 995 BC
1 Chronicles 17
Psalms 8, 113

Day 4
Psalms 24, 96, 97
Psalms 101, 105, 112
Psalms 146, 150

Day 5
2 Samuel 8
I Chronicles 18
Psalms 5, 23, 60
2 Samuel 9
     Mephibosheth
Psalm 98

Psalm 60: Amid many victories over the enemies of God, the setting of this psalm suggests that the army met with stiff resistance (vs. 1-3), and apparently even temporary defeat (vs. 9-10). The last statement shows David's hope and total trust in God's power: "With God we will gain the victory, and he will trample down our enemies" (v. 12 NIV).

Day 6
2 Samuel 10
1 Chronicles 19
Psalm 20
1 Chronicles 20
Psalms 9, 53

1 Chronicles 20: Dr. J. Vernon McGee sees the Chronicles as written from God's viewpoint. David's adultery was not mentioned here. God forgives repented sin and remembers it no more (Hebrews 8:12) (McGee).

Day 7
2 Samuel 11
     David and Bathsheba
2 Samuel 12
     Birth of Solomon: c. 990 BC
Psalms 51, 32

Samuel 12: Nathan's confrontation to David may have been as much as a year after his adultery, and David did not recognize his story as told. David spoke his own consequence to "repay...four sheep for the sheep" (Exodus 22:1). Four of David's sons died or were killed: Bathsheba's first son (unnamed), Amnon, Adonijah, and Absalom (McGee).

WEEK 19 READINGS

Day 1
2 Samuel 13-14

2 Samuel 13: Absalom fled to his grandfather, Talmai, who ruled the small Aramean city/state of Geshur near the Sea of Galilee (v. 37). When David was living with the Philistines he warred against the Geshurites (1 Samuel 27:8), and Absalom was born to a princess of Geshur (2 Samuel 3:3) (Beyer).

Day 2
2 Samuel 15
    Absalom's conspiracy
Psalms 3, 26
Psalms 55, 62

Day 3
2 Samuel 16-17
Psalms 13, 41
Psalm 63

2 Samuel 16: Nathan confronted David with prophecy: "This is what the Lord says, 'I am going to bring disaster on you from your own family: I will take your wives and give them to another before your very eyes, and he will sleep with them publicly. You acted in secret, but I will do this before all Israel and in broad daylight'" (2 Samuel 12:11; 16:22).

2 Samuel 17: Ahithophel was a faithful servant, and did his best for David. However, he was Bathsheba's grandfather (2 Samuel 11:3; 23:34), and

must have been in turmoil when David committed adultery and murdered Bathsheba's husband. When it looked like Absalom would take David's place, Ahithophel gave his advice (vs. 1-3) to the one he thought would be king. Then he saw his advice rejected, his victory plan would not happen, and Absalom would lose the battle. When David regained his kingdom, Ahithophel would be seen as a traitor, and most likely be put to death (Beyer).

Psalm 41: The close friend in verse 9 must have been Ahithophel, also called the Old Testament Judas. Both betrayed the masters they had faithfully served (2 Samuel 15:12, 31; 16:23; 17:1; John 13:18) (Halley).

Day 4
2 Samuel 18
David and Absalom's battle
Psalms 61, 69

Day 5
2 Samuel 19-20
Psalm 39

Day 6
2 Samuel 21
Psalms 4, 29, 31
Psalms 139, 144

Psalm 139: This beautiful Psalm is a song of praise to God's attributes, describing His omniscience (vs. 1-6), His omnipresence (vs. 7-18) and His omnipotence (vs. 19-24). The reactions to those attributes are stated in verses 6, 17-18, and 23-24. The first four verses say that God knows one's character, conduct, contemplations, and conversation (McGee; Rogers).

Day 7
2 Samuel 22
Psalms 18, 50

Week 20 Readings

Day 1
2 Samuel 24
     David's census: c. 980 BC
1 Chronicles 21
Psalm 38

1 Chronicles 21: Read verse one of chapter 22 with chapter 21. David's big sin (v. 8) may have been one of pride, trusting in numbers rather than in the Lord. The same events are explained different ways. For census numbers, Holman notes suggest that Chronicles lists swordsmen and 2 Samuel lists fighting men. Ellicott said all numbers were rounded: 800,000 Israelites, plus 288,000 (rounded to 300,000) of David's standing army (1 Chronicles 27:1-15) totals 1,100,000. Joab did not complete the census (1 Chronicles 27:24), and the tribes of Levi and Benjamin were not counted (Corduan; Ellicott, Vol. 3).

1 Chronicles 21: It is common to see different spellings for foreign names. In some early manuscripts Ornan is Orna (in Chronicles) and Araunah is Aran (in Samuel). The Jebusites (some of the original Canaanites) held Jerusalem until David captured them and Araunah/Ornan continued to live there. The price of silver (2 Samuel 24:24) seems too little and the price of gold (1 Chronicles 21:25) too much! The authors wrote of two different things. Samuel's may have been only the threshing floor, and the chronicler may have referred to the entire Mount Moriah–the place where Abraham offered Isaac, and where Solomon's temple would be built (2 Chronicles 3:1) (Ellicott, Vol. 3).

Day 2
Psalms 78, 88, 89

Day 3
1 Chronicles 22-24
>   David's charge to Solomon
Psalm 65

Day 4
1 Chronicles 25-26
Psalms 81, 92

Day 5
1 Chronicles 27-28
Psalm 30

Day 6
2 Samuel 23
1 Kings 1
>   Adonijah and Solomon: 970 BC
>   Events in the book of 1 Kings: c. 970-872 BC

2 Samuel 23 is a recap of David's elite army corps and a few special events during his lifetime, not just contemporary to the writing.

Day 7
1 Chronicles 29
>   Solomon's reign: 970-931 BC
Psalms 37, 118

1 Chronicles 29: There is division among scholars about the statement that Solomon was made king a second time (v. 22). Some believe David informally made Solomon king (23:1), after which Adonijah tried to take the throne (1 Kings 1:5). It was at this second time that King David made his choice known publicly (Corduan).

WEEK 21 READINGS

Day 1
1 Kings 2
Psalms 72, 73
Psalms 99, 149

1 Kings 2: Adonijah's request for Abishag was another attempt for kingship. Ancient kings took the former king's wives to solidify their position. Bathsheba may have sensed this threat to the throne, and passed the information on to Solomon with her request (Bowling).

Day 2
2 Chronicles 1: 970 BC
1 Kings 3
Psalm 45
Proverbs 31

1 Kings 3: Solomon's political marriage to an Egyptian princess may have made her an ambassador, able to ask for foreign wives and governmental representatives to be able to worship their own gods while in Israel (Bowling).

Day 3
Song of Songs 1-7: c. 970 BC

Scholars see four different interpretations for the Song of Songs, or Song of Solomon: (1) It declares wedded love and marriage to be a sacred institution. (2) It displays the love of God for Israel. Prophets called Israel the bride of Jehovah. (3) It shows the picture of the church as the bride of Christ. (4) It sets forth communion between Christ and the individual believer (McGee).

Day 4
Song of Songs 8
1 Kings 4-5
2 Chronicles 2

1 Kings 4: Daily provisions for Solomon have been considered enough for 20,000 persons. Solomon had a large harem with children and servants. The food may have been enough for his officials and military personnel, and possibly enough for the horses, which are numbered as 4000 in 2 Chronicles 9:25. These may have been stabled throughout the kingdom (Bowling).

1 Kings 4:29-34: Solomon was a political ruler, lecturer in botany and zoology, poet, scientist, businessman, moralist and preacher. Solomon's use of Hebrew made it an important world language, and he put God's truth into written word for the world. Noted wise men include Heman and Ethan (v. 31), who wrote Psalms 88 and 89. Solomon's reign from 970-931 BC suggests a possibility of being contemporary with Homer, who authored *The Iliad* and *The Odyssey*, and wrote about the Trojan horse in the battle of Troy. Homer's dates range from 1200 BC to 750 BC (Halley; Livingston; Biography.com).

Day 5
1 Kings 6: 966 BC
        Building of the temple
2 Chronicles 3
Psalm 104

2 Chronicles 3: The temple had many symbols of deity and worship. The curtain speaks of the humanity of Christ, and was torn in two from top to bottom at His crucifixion. The two pillars symbolized beauty (Psalm 27:4) and strength of worship. Strength speaks of salvation (Exodus 15:2a) (McGee).

Day 6
1 Kings 7
2 Chronicles 4
Psalm 148

Day 7
Proverbs 30
Proverbs 1-3: 970 BC

WEEK 22 READINGS

Day 1
Proverbs 4-8

Day 2
1 Kings 8
    Temple dedicated: 959 BC

Day 3
2 Chronicles 5
Psalms 95, 132
2 Chronicles 6

2 Chronicles 5: A pair of cymbals (v. 12) was found dating to the time of the kings of Judah. Small round bronze plates had a hole in the center for straps or threads to be fastened to the player's fingers. Bronze is flexible so it can produce high ringing sustained notes. Leaders of the music procession used cymbals, and they may have beat out the marching steps (Mazar, Vol. 4; Corduan).

2 Chronicles 5-6: The cloud, which filled the temple (5:14), revealed that God was pleased with what the people had done. Because of the cloud, their activities had to cease, and God's presence was then the focal point of worship (6:1, 4). For many years the cloud had been a guide, and now it came to rest inside the sanctuary, displaying God's presence and glory. But God's presence was not only in the temple. Solomon's prayer proclaimed God's presence is everywhere (6:18) (Corduan).

Day 4
2 Chronicles 7
Psalms 84, 87, 93
Psalms 127, 135, 136

Day 5
1 Kings 9
2 Chronicles 8
Proverbs 9-10

1 Kings 9: God appeared to Solomon and consecrated the temple as holy, a place for His name, His eyes, and His heart (v. 3). He proclaimed that He would dwell there, He would give His attention to it and look out from it, and His affections would be there. 1 Corinthians 6:19-20 says the believer's body is the dwelling place of the Holy Spirit. This is where God will be seen, will look out from, and where His affection will be felt by others. The believer's life will be a sanctuary for His name, His eyes, and His heart (Bowling).

2 Chronicles 8: Solomon's long association with Hiram of Tyre included frequent correspondence concerning current problems. Josephus indicated that the better solutions came from Solomon. The two developed a prosperous trade on the seas using ships Solomon had built, and experienced seamen provided by Hiram (Barabas).

Day 6
Proverbs 11-14

Day 7
Proverbs 15-18

Week 23 Readings

Day 1
Proverbs 19-22

Day 2
Proverbs 23, 24
Ecclesiastes 1-2: c. 935 BC

Day 3
2 Chronicles 9
Queen of Sheba's visit
1 Kings 10
Psalm 49

2 Chronicles 9: Old Testament evangelism was centered in Israel. The Queen of Sheba and kings of all nations sought Solomon's wisdom (v. 23) and he prayed for God to answer the prayers of foreigners who would come to the beautiful temple to pray. Later Naaman came to Israel and believed in God (Bowling; Livingston).

Day 4
Ecclesiastes 3-6

Day 5
Ecclesiastes 7-10

Day 6
Ecclesiastes 11-12
1 Kings 11

Ecclesiastes 12:1-7: The Ecclesiastes poem of the aged has various interpretations. "The sun and the light are darkened" brings death, or it could refer to eyesight that no longer sees the light clearly. "The guardians of the house" are hands that "tremble," and "the strong men" are legs that still support a stooped back. "Grinders cease because they are few" (ESV), are teeth; the eyes are the "windows," and they "see dimly." The "doors at the street are shut" as hearing fades, yet the "sound of a bird" may awaken one in the morning. "Daughters of song grow faint" when one can no longer sing well. Being "afraid of heights" makes one fear falling, and "dangers on the road" might be criminals with easy prey, or it may refer to no longer enjoying travel. White hair is like "the almond tree blossoms" and the "grasshopper loses its spring" when romance is gone. "Mourners will walk around" missing the one who "is headed to his eternal home." The "silver cord" is the spinal cord, the "gold bowl" the head, the "jar" the lungs and the "wheel" is the heart. Another interpretation is that silver and gold indicate life is precious. (McGee; Garrett).

1 Kings 11: Solomon's "foreign women drew him into sin" (Nehemiah 13:26). All the world came to hear Solomon, but his apostasy amid luxury is a pitiful story (Bowling; Halley; Livingston).

Day 7
2 Chronicles 10
      Rehoboam's reign: 931-913 BC
2 Chronicles 11
1 Kings 12
      Kingdom divided: 931 BC
      Jeroboam's reign in Israel: 931-910 BC
      See Appendices E and F

2 Chronicles 10: "Scorpion" (v. 11) was a nickname for spiked and barbed whips, a common disciplinary instrument (Mazar, Vol. 2; Corduan).

WEEK 24 READINGS

Day 1
1 Kings 13-14

Day 2
2 Chronicles 12-13
> Pharaoh Shishak's invasion: 926 BC
1 Kings 15

2 Chronicles 12: Shishak inscribed his record of Palestinian wars and 180 captured cities on a temple wall in Karnak. Jerusalem is not listed. Rehoboam humbled himself, and God delivered Jerusalem from Shishak (v. 7). However, Rehoboam gave him Solomon's objects of gold. Shishak's mummy was found, and some of this gold may have been used on his silver sarcophagus, which was encased in solid gold (Mazar, Vol. 2 and 4; Halley).

Day 3
2 Chronicles 14
> Asa's reign in Judah: 911-870 BC
Psalm 66
2 Chronicles 15-16

Day 4
1 Kings 16
> Baasha's reign in Israel: 909-886 BC
> Ahab's reign in Israel: 874-853 BC
2 Chronicles 17
> Jehoshaphat's reign in Judah: 873-848 BC
Psalm 71

1 Kings 16: The length of reign for Tibni is not declared. After Zimri's suicide, Tibni and Omri were in civil war for five years and each may have ruled their followers until Tibni died (v. 21) (Bowling).

Day 5
1 Kings 17
> Elijah's ministry: 870-845 BC

Psalm 111
1 Kings 18
> Contest on Mt. Carmel

1 Kings 18: Jezebel was the daughter of Ethbaal, king of the Sidonians and high priest of Baal, the storm god. People may have believed the idol could provide fire through lightning. The contest between God and the prophets of Baal as well as the contest between God and the gods of Egypt at the time of Moses could be summed up with Martin Luther's quote: "one with God is a majority." God said, "there was no one like Ahab, who devoted himself to do what was evil in the Lord's sight" (21:25) (McGee; Bowling).

1 Kings 18: Death of false prophets (v. 40) was law (Deuteronomy 13). These prophets sacrificed infants to Baal. Many jars with infant remains were found at a cemetery near Megiddo. This is where the battle of Armageddon will be fought (Revelation 16:16) (Bowling; Halley).

Day 6
1 Kings 19-20
> Ahab's victory: 855 BC

Day 7
1 Kings 21
> Ahab and Naboth's vineyard

2 Chronicles 18

Week 25 Readings

Day 1
1 Kings 22
      Chapter events: 870-852 BC
      Review of events of 2 Chronicles 17-20
2 Chronicles 19

Day 2
2 Chronicles 20
      Jehoshaphat revival: 853 BC
Psalms 44, 48, 83

2 Chronicles 20: Jehoshaphat gave thanks and praised the Lord before victory (vs. 6, 20-22) as was David's example (Psalm 18:3).

Day 3
2 Kings 1-2
      Elijah's chariot of fire: c. 845 BC
2 Kings 3

2 Kings 2: Elisha's request for a double portion of Elijah's spirit (v. 9) was not arrogant. He had been called Elijah's heir (1 Kings 19:19-21). A firstborn son's inheritance was two shares of the legacy (Deuteronomy 21:17) (Bowling).

2 Kings 2: 23-24: God's judgment on "small boys" or "little children" (v. 23 KJV) seems extremely harsh. The same Hebrew word is used for Isaac at 28, Joseph at 39, and his slightly younger brother Benjamin with ten sons. This was scoffing and ridicule (2 Peter 3:3-4) (McGee).

Day 4
2 Chronicles 21
2 Kings 4
>   Elisha's miracles

2 Chronicles 21: Elijah was taken in the chariot of fire in the eighteenth year of Jehoshaphat's reign. This letter (v. 12) was true prophecy, written before his translation. Another explanation for the timing is that Jehoram may have co-reigned with his father, Jehoshaphat (McGee).

Day 5
2 Kings 5
>   Naaman
2 Kings 6-7

Day 6
2 Kings 8
>   Chapter events: 853-841 BC
2 Kings 9
>   Jehu's reign in Israel: 841-814 BC

2 Kings 8: The account of the Shunamite woman and her property (vs. 1-8) took place before Gehazi was leprous and out of service to Elisha (5:27).

Day 7
2 Kings 10
2 Chronicles 22
2 Kings 11
Psalm 117

2 Kings 11: Athaliah had a thirst for power strong enough to kill anyone who might claim the throne. In this, Satan almost succeeded in cutting off David's line, prophesied to be the one through whom God would send the Messiah (NIV).

WEEK 26 READINGS

Day 1
2 Chronicles 23-24
> Joash's reign in Judah: 835-796 BC
2 Kings 12

Day 2
2 Kings 13
2 Chronicles 25
> Amaziah's reign in Judah: 796-767 BC

Day 3
2 Kings 14
> Jeroboam II's reign in Israel: 793-753 BC
Jonah 1-2: c. 781 BC
Psalm 116

Jonah 1: Nineveh, Assyria's capital, used torture in warfare. Tarshish is thought to be in the far southwest part of Spain. Phoenician sailors traded between Egypt and Spain, and may have used ships with both sails and fifty or sixty rowers (Sprinkle; Halley; McGee; Ellicott, Vol. 5; Mazar, Vol. 3).

Day 4
Jonah 3-4
2 Chronicles 26
> Uzziah (Azariah)'s reign in Judah: 792-740 BC
Amos 1-2
> Amos' prophecy: c. 765-754 BC

Jonah 3: Nineveh was over 500 miles northeast of Caanan. A three-day's journey suggests the metropolis had a circumference of about 60 miles (assuming a day's journey was 18 to 23 miles). Forty days may refer to a period of testing or judgment (Numbers 14:34; I Kings 19; Luke 4:2) (Sprinkle; Halley).

Jonah 4: About the time of Jonah's visit, the king took tribute from Israel. Jonah's influence on Nineveh was profound, and he may have been instrumental in Israel's recovery of lost territory (2 Kings 14:25). Archeologists Rich, Botla and Layard discovered a sacred Jonah Mound with no excavation allowed. His tomb could either be here, or at the traditional Gath-hepher site. Inhabitants not knowing left from right (v. 11) may refer to children, then a population of 600,000 to a million. Or it may indicate spiritual and moral immaturity (Sprinkle; Ellicott; Halley; McGee).

2 Chronicles 26: Uzziah co-reigned with his father Amaziah, and son Jotham during the years of leprosy (Bowling).

Amos 1-2: God's statement "for three crimes, even four" (1:3), may mean seven–God's number of completeness for required judgment. It could also mean counting to three–at four you have stepped over the line (Garrett; McGee).

Day 5
Amos 3-6

Day 6
Amos 7-9
Hosea 1-2
       Hosea's prophecy: c. 758-725 BC

Amos 8: The total sun eclipse (v. 9) recorded on a clay tablet at Nineveh was on June 15, 763 BC, and provides a fixed point for Old Testament chronology (Mazar, Vol. 3).

Day 7
2 Kings 15
     Chapter events: 792-735 BC
Isaiah 1-2
     Isaiah's prophecy: c. 740-698 BC

Isaiah prophesied during the reigns of Uzziah and Jotham (1-6), Ahaz (7-14), and Hezekiah (chapter 15 and on). Isaiah uses prophetic perfect, a method of writing as if something has already happened, but with events still in the future (Longman III).

WEEK 27 READINGS

Day 1
Isaiah 3-6
> God's call, Uzziah's death: 740 BC

Isaiah 5: God is sovereign over the nations. When He blows the "whistle" (v. 26), they respond: the lion was Assyria's icon of royalty (v. 29); and Babylon gladly came later (chapter 13) (Longman III).

Isaiah 6: To get people's attention, God repeated three times, "Holy, holy, holy" (v. 3). Holiness is the preeminent character of God (MacArthur).

Day 2
Hosea 3-5
2 Chronicles 27
> Jotham's reign in Judah: 750-734 BC
Micah 1-2
> Micah's prophecy: c. 738-698 BC

Hosea compared Israel's relationship to God with the marriage relationship: allow no rivals (Clendenen).

2 Chronicles 27: Jotham reigned after Uzziah was stricken with leprosy (26:21). A few years before the end of Jotham's reign, his son, Ahaz, became king. Co-regency rarely mentioned, helps to explain dates that do not seem compatible (Corduan; Bowling).

Day 3
2 Chronicles 28
     Ahaz' reign in Judah: 735-716 BC
2 Kings 16
Isaiah 7

Day 4
Isaiah 8-10

Isaiah 9: The "day of Midian" (v. 4) refers to the day of Gideon with his 300 chosen soldiers (Judges 7:7) (Longman III).

Isaiah 9:10: "The bricks have fallen, but we will rebuild," was a statement of defiance against God's judgment, as if to say, we will do it stronger and better ourselves. After 9-11 America's highest officials quoted portions of that verse. With parallel timing and corresponding actions, "it was happening and is happening" in ancient Israel and in America (Jonathan Cahn in *The Harbinger*).

Day 5
Isaiah 11-13
Hosea 6-8

Isaiah 11: The stump of Jesse (v. 1) indicates that the Davidic kingdom was halted, but a shoot (Jesus) will come up from that stump, and revive the royal line of David when He comes again (NIV).

Day 6
Hosea 9-10
2 Kings 17
     Hoshea's reign in Israel: 732-722 BC
     Deportation of Israel by Assyrians: 722 BC
Psalm 80

2 Kings 17: God permitted Israel to go into captivity because of their disobedience, doubt, and defiance. After Shalmaneser took the northern tribes into captivity, he brought foreigners to the land (v. 24), which

intermarried with the few remaining Israelites, and the Samaritan race was born (McGee).

Day 7
Hosea 11
Isaiah 14: 716 BC
2 Chronicles 29
      Hezekiah's reign in Judah: 716-687 BC

Week 28 Readings

Day 1
2 Chronicles 30
Psalms 123, 125
Hosea 12-14

2 Chronicles 30: Hezekiah's invitations to the Northern Kingdom for the Passover celebration may have been an effort to unite the divided kingdom. Some people mocked, but some attended. It was also an evangelistic effort as some foreigners came (Corduan).

Day 2
Micah 3-7

Micah 5: Bethlehem Ephrathah (v. 2) included both modern and ancient names of the prophesied place of Jesus' birthplace (Genesis 35:19; Matthew 2:1,6). Verses two and three are about Jesus' first coming; the remainder of chapter 5 is about His second coming (Ellicott, Vol. 5).

Day 3
2 Chronicles 31
Psalms 128, 134
Proverbs 25-27

2 Chronicles 31: Revival took place during Hezekiah's 29-year reign. The Bible includes a lot of messages and prophecies that took place during those years–literature that is here and into the next two weeks.

Psalm 128: The Psalmist's family discussion named sons "like young olive trees around your table" (v. 3). Olive trees take a long time, up to 15 years, to bear fruit. They can then bear good, not bitter, fruit for generations. So after years of cultivating, or with children, after years of investing in loving nurture, good fruit may be found (King).

Day 4
Proverbs 28-29
Isaiah 15-17

Isaiah 16: The prediction of Moab's destruction was dated for three years "as a hired worker counts years" (v. 14). It was customary for an employment contract to be for three years as found in the Code of Hammurabi and hinted at in Deuteronomy 15:18, though this was related to slavery. Scholars believe the fall of Moab came with Assyrian Sargon's campaign about three years later in 718 BC (Mazar, Vol. 3; Longman III).

Day 5
Isaiah 18-22

Day 6
Isaiah 23-27

Isaiah 23: Tyre, an island city of southern Phoenicia had developed and then controlled sea trade. It was a wealthy city, and "became the marketplace of the nations" (v. 3 NIV). Its people were proud, and very evil. Other prophets such as Jeremiah, Ezekiel, Joel, Amos and Zechariah rebuked Tyre with prophecies of destruction. The 70 years (v. 15) may have taken place during the time of the Assyrian or Babylonian captivities of Israel and Judah. Tyre was one of the most famous cities of the ancient world (Longman III; NIV).

Day 7
Isaiah 28-30

Week 29 Readings

Day 1
Isaiah 31
Psalms 82, 94
Isaiah 32-34

Isaiah 33: The "destroyer" (v. 1) was Sennacherib of Assyria. He attacked after Hezekiah had given much to prevent an attack (2 Kings 18:13-16), but Sennacherib broke the treaty (v. 8). Isaiah prophesied that as Sennacherib brought terror, he would be terrorized (2 Kings 19:27-28), and God would give the victory (Ellicott, Vol. 4).

Day 2
Isaiah 35
Isaiah 40-42

Isaiah 40: Isaiah prophesied until about ten years before Hezekiah's reign ended, so the last 27 chapters, must have been Isaiah's messages during the good days of Hezekiah's reign, before his illness and the Assyrian conflict in chapters 36 through 39.

Day 3
Isaiah 43-45

Isaiah 44: Cyrus was named around 700 BC (v. 28), 150 years before his time, and Isaiah prophesied that he would rebuild Jerusalem and the temple. These were not destroyed until 586 BC, and Cyrus' decree came about 50 years later in 538 BC (Ezra 1:1-2). Jeremiah, Ezekiel, and other prophets around this time prophesied about what God would do, and history declares that it came true. Halley lists ten of Isaiah's prophecies that were fulfilled in his lifetime, thirteen general predictions fulfilled after his time, and nineteen prophecies about the Messiah (Halley; Moorehead; Longman III).

Day 4
Isaiah 46-49

Isaiah 48: Many prophecies were about heathen nations, but God's own people (vs. 1-6) were rebuked for being idolatrous, honoring Him only with their lips, and making up their own rules. The people accused Isaiah of being unpatriotic when he rebuked their sinfulness (Ellicott, Vol. 4).

Day 5
Isaiah 50-53

Isaiah 53: A shepherd wrote of his sheep as not stupid, but stubborn, instinctively heading for bushes, hills or farms, and often getting into trouble (v. 6). They need to listen to the shepherd who calls them back to safety (Darmani).

Isaiah 53: Not suffering for His own sin, Jesus was silent and went willingly to the cross. This prophecy (vs. 7-8) was written 700 years before Calvary (Halley).

Day 6
Isaiah 54-58

Day 7
Isaiah 59-62

Isaiah 61: Jesus read these words (vs. 1-2a) in the synagogue (Luke 4:18-19), stopping after "to proclaim the year of the Lord's favor" (v. 2a). These phrases described His first coming. The "day of our God's vengeance" (v. 2b) will happen at His second coming as described in the rest of this chapter and the next (NIV).

Week 30 Readings

Day 1
Isaiah 63-66: c. 698 BC

Day 2
Isaiah 38
> Hezekiah's illness and recovery
2 Kings 20
Isaiah 39
2 Chronicles 32

2 Chronicles 32: Hezekiah chiseled a 1,680-foot tunnel (v. 30) in a winding path from the Gihon spring to a pool in Jerusalem. Rock was cut with picks from each end until workers met in the middle. A Hebrew inscription of 15 by 30 inches lists engineering calculations. When Assyrians invaded Judah, Hezekiah closed off their access to the spring (v. 4) (Bowling; Mazar, Vol. 2, 4).

Day 3
2 Kings 18
Isaiah 36
Psalm 77

Day 4
Psalm 120
2 Kings 19
> Hezekiah with Assyrian letter: 701 BC
Isaiah 37

Day 5
Psalms 46, 47, 76
Psalms 121, 129
2 Chronicles 33
   Manasseh's reign in Judah: 697-643 BC

2 Chronicles 33: The time of Manasseh's birth may be in one of two ways. Ellicott suggests that Hezekiah reigned 41 years, not 29, and that Manasseh co-reigned with him from his birth. Bowling suggests that Manasseh was born before Hezekiah's extra years, and co-regency began when Manasseh was twelve. He began sole rule in his early 20's. Two Assyrian kings list Manasseh as a vassal who supplied troops for Ashurbanipal's battle against Thebes in Egypt about 663 BC. When Assyria captured Manasseh, he repented, and was allowed to go back to Jerusalem where he tried to encourage people to follow God. Hezekiah is called one of Judah's best kings (2 Kings 18:5; 2 Chronicles 31:20), and Manasseh one of the worst, more wicked than the heathen (I Kings 21:9-11) (Bowling; Ellicott, Vol. 3; Corduan).

Day 6
2 Kings 21
Nahum 1-3
   Nahum's prophecy: c. 658-615 BC

Nahum prophesied to Nineveh about a hundred years after Jonah's visit. The people had returned to their sinful ways, and Assyrian artists carved their atrocities in stone. Nineveh fell about 20 years after Nahum's prediction. The site was lost until archaeologists, Rich, Botla and Layard found the ruins. Sennacherib's palace was the size of three large city blocks. It contained his descendant, Ashurbanipal's library of 100,000 volumes, now partly in a British museum (Halley; Mazar, Vol. 2).

Day 7
Zephaniah 1-3
   Zephaniah's prophecy: c. 640-626 BC
Joel 1
   Joel's prophecy: between 722 and 605 BC

Joel: Scholars give the time for Joel's prophecy from 835 BC to after 445 BC. Bowling communicated in personal conversation, that Joel's prophecy was after the deportation in 722 BC, but before 605 BC. Joel is placed here after Manasseh and Amon's reigns.

WEEK 31 READINGS

Day 1
Joel 2-3
2 Kings 22

Day 2
2 Chronicles 34
     Josiah's reign in Judah: 641-609 BC
     Book of the Law found: 623 BC
Psalm 67
Jeremiah 1
     Jeremiah's prophecy: 627- c. 580 BC

2 Chronicles 34: Josiah made his revival public: "He had all those present… agree…to serve the Lord" (vs. 32-33). Josiah's heart was right, and he worked hard to remove the idols, but the people's service may have been only outward, while inwardly idolatrous.

Jeremiah 1: Like Isaiah, Jeremiah was to preach although people would not listen (vs. 17-19; 7:27). The almond tree (v. 11) was called a waker, because it was the first to wake (bloom) after winter. Jeremiah was to be a waker, an alarm clock to awaken the nation from their godless, luxurious life style (McGee).

Day 3
Jeremiah 2-3

Day 4
Jeremiah 4-6

Jeremiah 4: Jeremiah used common examples in his prophecies, and he seemed confused by them (v. 10). He claimed Jerusalem prettied herself for nothing. As early as the time of Jezebel (2 Kings 9:30) women dressed up using a silver-white metallic base for eye-makeup with black powder on the eyelids (v. 30) (Kaiser).

Day 5
Jeremiah 7-8
Temple Gate Sermon: 621 BC

Jeremiah 7-8: The temple gate sermon during Josiah's eighteenth year after temple cleansing included a variety of illustrations not common today. Shiloh (7:12, 14) was where the tabernacle and the Ark of the Covenant had been set up, but destroyed over 400 years earlier by the Philistines (1 Samuel 4:1-11; Psalm 78:60-64). The Queen of Heaven (7:18) and Molech at Topheth (2 Kings 23:10) were idols from Manasseh's reign (1 Kings 21:5). After the Nazarite vow was fulfilled, the long hair was cut and burned (7:29). The false prophets were like quack doctors (8:11-12). The balm in Gilead (8:22) was a medicinal balm from the balsam tree applied to wounds for healing (McGee; Kaiser).

Day 6
Jeremiah 9-11

Jeremiah 11: People from Jeremiah's hometown of Anathoth plotted and schemed against him (v. 21) because he pronounced coming disaster (McGee; Kaiser).

Day 7
Jeremiah 12
2 Chronicles 35
Josiah's Passover celebration

2 Chronicles 35: Despite no genuine change of people's hearts with Josiah's reforms, and though people conspired against him (Jeremiah 11:9), the people loved, followed and mourned for him (v. 24). "As long as he lived,

they did not fail to follow the Lord," (2 Chronicles 34:33 NIV). God said, "Before him there was no king like him who turned to the Lord with all his mind and with all his heart and with all his strength according to all the law of Moses, and no one like him arose after him" (2 Kings 23:25).

WEEK 32 READINGS

Day 1
2 Kings 23
        Jehoiakim's reign in Judah: 609-598 BC
Jeremiah 14

2 Kings 23: Josiah followed the Law, but national repentance did not continue past his reign. His sons, Jehoahaz (Shallum) and Eliakim (Jehoiakim) were not changed. God could not turn from his fury, but He said, "If you return, I will restore you" (Jeremiah 15:19). Josiah's reforms set up the religious life that existed after return from exile many years later (Bowling; Corduan).

Day 2
Jeremiah 15-17

Day 3
Jeremiah 18-20

Jeremiah 19-20: This is not the only time cannibalism is mentioned in scripture (19:9). It occurred when Samaria was besieged (2 Kings 6:28-29), and at the Babylonian siege of 586 BC (Lamentations 2:20; 4:10). Josephus wrote that this also happened when the Romans captured Jerusalem in AD 70. Persecution has often begun with organized religion (20:1-2). Pashhur was a priest in charge of keeping order at the temple. Part of the priest's duty was to put false prophets into stocks and neck-irons (29:26). Jeremiah called Pashhur a terrorist (Kaiser).

Day 4
Jeremiah 26
Habakkuk 1-3
> Habakkuk's prophecy: c. 608- 598 BC

Habakkuk 1-3: Rather than speaking to the people for God, Habakkuk spoke to God for the people's sake. The speed, brutality, and efficiency of the coming Babylonian army were characterized by the leopard, wolf, and eagle or vulture (1:8). Babylonians did unspeakable things and worshipped their army, as effective as a fisherman who worshipped his nets (1:16). Habakkuk was frightened with the news of coming tragedy. Yet he rejoiced and praised the Lord, his strength, and said he could be on the mountaintop (3:16-19) (Sprinkle; NIV).

Habakkuk 2: The key to the book and the whole Bible is the just (righteous) will live by his faith (v. 4). This verse is quoted in the three doctrinal books, Romans, Galatians and Hebrews (McGee).

Day 5
Daniel 1: 605 BC
> Nebuchadnezzar's reign in Babylon: 605-562 BC
Jeremiah 25, 46

Daniel 1: Most likely Daniel and his friends grew up during the time of Josiah's reforms, and it may have seemed as if his work of cleansing the nation was fruitless. But Daniel and his friends influenced evil kings for years. Daniel's influence may have lasted into the New Testament era with the magi coming to worship the Christ (Walvoord).

Day 6
Jeremiah 47-48
Jeremiah 35

Day 7
Jeremiah 36
>   Letter to Jehoiakim: 605-604 BC
Daniel 2
>   Nebuchadnezzar's dream: 604 BC

Daniel lived in one of the most heathen countries in the world, but he was prime minister under seven kings in two empires. The four world empires from Nebuchadnezzar's dream ruled from the days of Daniel to the time of Christ: Babylonia, Persia, Greece, and Rome (Graham; Halley).

WEEK 33 READINGS

Day 1
Jeremiah 45
Jeremiah 22
2 Kings 24
> Zedekiah's reign in Judah: 597-586 BC
Psalm 137

Day 2
Jeremiah 13
Jeremiah 49

Jeremiah 49: Edom occupied a large territory in the mountains. The capital, Petra, was "in the clefts of the rock" (v. 16), which led them to believe they could not be conquered. They were cruel (v. 16), proud of their wisdom (Obadiah 8), and rich from copper and iron mines. God indicated He would restore the fortunes of some other nations (vs. 6, 39), but not Edom (vs. 17-18). Check Petra on the Internet for pictures of rock-hewn dwellings.

Jeremiah 49: God called Damascus "the town that brings Me joy" (v. 25). Damascus was the capital of Aram, and along with Babylon, attacked Jerusalem. Nebuchadnezzar defeated Damascus in 605 BC, and God destroyed Aram completely as prophesied (Amos 1:4-5). Damascus has since been occupied continuously (NIV; Tenney; Kaiser).

Day 3
Jeremiah 50
Jeremiah 23

Jeremiah 23: Judah's shepherds (kings, priests, prophets, spiritual and civic leaders) led the people astray (v. 1). The false prophets were of low morals and character (v. 14). They either made up their own prophecies (v. 16), or repeated the falsities of other prophets (v. 30). God said He had not called them (vs. 21-22). True and false prophets are as different as grain and straw (v. 28), either nourishing or useless. God raised up good shepherds (vs. 3-4), like Zerubbabel, Ezra, and Nehemiah, and continues to raise up ministers until Christ comes to reign (v. 5) (Kaiser; NIV).

Day 4
Jeremiah 29
Jeremiah 24
Jeremiah 27-28

Day 5
Jeremiah 51
Ezekiel 1
> Ezekiel's prophecy: c. 593-570 BC

Ezekiel 1: "In the thirtieth year" (v. 1) is likely Ezekiel's 30th birthday, the age when priests began their service, and the date of Ezekiel's call to ministry. Other dates given throughout the book relate to this deportation of April 22, 597 BC. The creatures (vs. 5-11) signify world control. These are the creatures in Revelation chapter four (Rooker; NIV).

Day 6
Ezekiel 2-5

Ezekiel 2-3: Ezekiel was taken to Babylon during the second siege along with Jehoiachin and 10,000 others (2 Kings 24:13-15), who settled near Nippur by the Chebar River (1:3). Like Moses to Pharaoh, and like Isaiah and Jeremiah, Ezekiel was asked to speak to the people whether or not they listened (2:7; 3:5-9). As for Ezekiel, he found God's word as sweet as honey (3:3) (NIV).

Day 7
Ezekiel 6-8: 591 BC

WEEK **34** READINGS

Day 1
Ezekiel 9-11
Psalms 42, 43

Ezekiel 11: The glory of God left from the mountain east of Jerusalem (v. 23), the same direction of King David's flight from Absalom (2 Samuel 15:23). Jesus ascended from this mountain, and promised to return there (Zechariah 14:4; Acts 1:9-12) (Rooker).

Day 2
Ezekiel 12-14

Ezekiel 14: In the midst of corruption, Noah, Job and Daniel (v. 14) were recognized as examples of moral and spiritual responsibility. They were able to save others: Noah, his family (Genesis 6:18); Job, his companions from consequences (Job 42:7-8); and Daniel, his friends (Daniel 2:17-18) (Rooker; Ellicott, Vol. 5).

Day 3
Ezekiel 15-16

Ezekiel 16: In the ancient world baby girls were often abandoned (vs. 3-5). Later God chose Jerusalem, spreading the "garment over you" (v. 8), designating a marriage proposal calling Israel his bride. Israel left that first love, became idolatrous, sacrificed little ones to idols (v. 20), and despised the covenant (v. 59) (McGee).

Day 4
Ezekiel 17-19

Ezekiel 17: The great eagle (v. 3) was Nebuchadnezzar, king of Babylon; Jehoiachin was the topmost twig that had been taken to Babylon six years earlier. The seed was Zedekiah (v.5), and the second great eagle (v. 7) was Egypt's Pharaoh upon whom Zedekiah leaned. Zedekiah was taken to Babylon five years later. The tender twig or sprig (vs. 22-24) was the Messiah that God would later plant in the royal family (Rooker; Halley).

Day 5
Ezekiel 20-21: 590 BC

Ezekiel 21: King Nebuchadnezzar was God's drawn sword (v. 3), which was a typical way to refer to warfare. The strikes of the sword (v. 14) may be the three attacks and deportations of Jerusalem by the Babylonians in 605, 597, and 586 BC. Removal of the turban (v. 26) meant the removal of priests and kings from Judah. The turban, was also a setting for the royal crown, and was not to be worn again until the coming of Messiah (Rooker).

Day 6
Daniel 3
    The fiery furnace: 589 BC
Ezekiel 22
Psalm 102

Daniel 3: Babylonian records mention a revolt in the tenth year of Nebuchadnezzar's reign, and it is possible that this statue could have been a test of loyalty. Daniel was at the king's court (2:49). Scholars think the furnace was built on a hill with openings at both side and top. It may have been used to smelt the gold for the statue. After acknowledging Israel's God as the greatest (3:29), Nebuchadnezzar continued to worship his idols (Rydelnick).

Ezekiel 22: The names of the immoral sisters represent Samaria and Jerusalem, and had meanings that referred to tents, perhaps recalling when Israel lived in tents in the desert and met God in the tabernacle, a tent. The prostitution (v. 5) represents idolatry and alliances with heathen nations. An obelisk of Shalmaneser III shows Jehu bowing before him in 841 BC (Rooker).

Day 7
Ezekiel 23-24

    Death of Ezekiel's wife: 588 BC

Week 35 Readings

Day 1
Jeremiah 30-31

Jeremiah 30: This message in the final days of the siege of Jerusalem includes medical language to show that sin is terminal (vs. 12-15), yet it tells of a bright future—one still to come (Kaiser).

Day 2
Jeremiah 37: 588 BC
Jeremiah 32

Jeremiah 32: Jeremiah was imprisoned at least four times in different ways because of his prophecies. Siege ramps were in place (v. 24) at the time of his land purchase/redemption (v. 9). Silver ingots used as money from Jeremiah's time were found in a cooking pot under a house floor in En-gedi. The earthen storage jar for documents (v. 14) was the kind in which Dead Sea Scrolls were sealed. This land purchase was a sign that the people would return (Kaiser).

Day 3
Jeremiah 33-34
Psalm 85
Jeremiah 21

Jeremiah 34: The ritual of ratifying the covenant with the calf (vs. 18-20) followed the ceremony that God engaged in with Abraham a thousand years earlier (Genesis 15:10, 17) (Myers; Kaiser).

Day 4
Jeremiah 38
Lamentations 3
Ezekiel 25

Day 5
Ezekiel 26-28

Ezekiel 28: Lucifer's fall was depicted as God spoke to Satan through the king of Tyre (vs. 12-19).

Day 6
Ezekiel 29-31

Ezekiel 29-31: The horn (29:21) symbolizes strength, and refers to the Messiah and His power over Israel's enemies in the end times. Egypt, once the highest of civilizations, and Pharaoh, a majestic symbol of royalty (31:2), were brought to the lowest place (29:15) because of unbelief (Rooker).

Day 7
Jeremiah 39
        Fall of Jerusalem: 588-586 BC
Lamentations 4
Obadiah 1: c. 586 BC

Jeremiah 39: Two years of siege was a long time, and much happened during that time as further readings reveal. So tragic was the fall of Jerusalem that it is recorded four times in scripture: 2 Kings 25; 2 Chronicles 36; Jeremiah 39, and 52.

Obadiah wrote shortly after the fall of Jerusalem (v. 11), and after Edom had helped capture and deliver Israelites to the Babylonians (v. 14). Edom would suffer for mistreating God's people, and the nation was in ruins within a hundred years (ESV).

WEEK 36 READINGS

Day 1
Jeremiah 52: 588- c. 561 BC
2 Kings 25: 586 BC
Psalm 79

Jeremiah 52: The year 586 BC is prominent in this chapter. God could no longer hold back His judgment because of Zedekiah's wickedness (vs. 2-3). King Jehoiachin's release from captivity in Babylon (v. 31) came after almost 40 years. Documents from Nebuchadnezzar's palace show that Jehoiachin received eight times the rations of other prisoners. At the time he had five sons, who also received rations. Jehoiachin (also called Jeconiah or Coniah) is in Mary's ancestry (Matthew 1:11) (Kaiser; Mazar, Vol. 3; McGee).

Day 2
2 Chronicles 36
Lamentations 1-2

2 Chronicles 36 covers over seventy years, and reviews times beginning with King Jehoahaz in 609 BC (2 Kings 23). The events of Cyrus of Persia (v. 22) are at the end of next week's readings.

Day 3
Jeremiah 40-41
      Gedaliah assassinated: 585 BC
Psalm 74
Lamentations 5

Day 4
Jeremiah 42-43
Ezekiel 32

Jeremiah 43: Jewish rebels, who did not believe Jeremiah, carried him and Baruch to Egypt near to Goshen (v. 7) (McGee).

Day 5
Ezekiel 33: 585 BC
Jeremiah 44: 580 BC

Ezekiel 33: The message beginning here was delivered the night before the news of the fall of Jerusalem in 586 arrived (vs. 21-22). The courier bringing news may have been in transit for five or six months. Ezekiel's message included the why of captivity—their sins. Later Ezekiel told them how to live in captivity, and gave them hope for future restoration (Ellicott, Vol. 5).

Day 6
Ezekiel 34-36

Ezekiel 36: God's declaration of cleansing Israel from all iniquities and making it like the Garden of Eden (vs. 33-36) will be a miracle of the millennium. The land of Israel, originally called a land flowing with milk and honey (Exodus 3:8), lost its fertility because of the peoples' disobedience and rebellion (Deuteronomy 11:13-17) (Rooker).

Day 7
Ezekiel 37-39

Ezekiel 38: Gog (v. 2) seems to serve as a symbol of evil, and of the forces of anti-christ. The invasion of Gog is mentioned in Revelation 19 and 20, and it could be that Gog represents the beast and Satan (Rooker).

Several secular persons and events arose around these times. In 582 BC, the Isthmian games began on the Isthmus of Corinth, and were held every two years, both the year before and the year after the Olympic Games, which had been held for almost 200 years. By 570 BC, Aesop, a slave of Xanthus of Samos, was credited with collecting and/or creating fables. Confucius, the Chinese philosopher, teacher and political figure lived from c. 551 BC to 479 BC (Biography.com; Wikipedia.org).

Week 37 Readings

Day 1
Daniel 4

> Nebuchadnezzar's pride; insanity: 573-566 BC

Ezekiel 40

> Vision of the new temple: c. 572 BC

Daniel 4: Nebuchadnezzar's insanity may have been boanthropy, a very rare mental illness in which people believe they are cattle, but are able to understand what has happened. Walvoord reported on a 1946 case of a twenty-year old in a British mental institution who wandered about outside, and ate only grass, not any institutional food. The only physical changes noted were lengthened hair and coarse, thickened fingernails (Rydelnick; Walvoord).

About this time, Buddha (c. 563-483 BC) said, "All we are is the result of all we have thought." Perhaps he knew of Solomon's proverb "For as he thinketh in his heart, so is he" (Proverbs 23:7 KJV) (Platt).

Day 2
Ezekiel 41-43

Day 3
Ezekiel 44-45

Day 4
Ezekiel 46-48

Ezekiel 47: The future blessing on the area of the Arabah is that when its water "enters the sea, the sea of foul water, the water of the sea becomes fresh" (v. 8). This foul water is the Dead Sea, six times saltier than the ocean, and in which nothing can live (Rooker; NIV).

Day 5
Daniel 7
Vision of four beasts: 548 BC
Daniel 8: 538 BC

Daniel 8: This prophetic vision identifies Alexander the Great, the goat (v. 5) and Antiochus Epiphanes (v. 9), who overthrew the priest and looted the temple in the second century BC (Weathers).

Day 6
Daniel 5
Handwriting on the wall: 538 BC
Daniel 9

Daniel 5: Belshazzar, the last Babylonian king, ruled from 548-538 BC, co-regent with Nabonidus for part of his reign. Daniel would have been in his mid-sixties when he was made the third ruler (Weathers).

Daniel 9: Xerxes, or Ahasuerus (v. 1), was not the same king who crowned Queen Esther about 50 years later. Ahasuerus may have been a Persian royal name (NIV).

Day 7
Ezra 1-2: 538 BC
Daniel 6
The lions' den: 536 BC

Ezra 1: Cyrus was king of Media-Persia from c. 559 to 530 BC with Darius the Mede (Daniel 9:1) as his governor for two years over declining Babylonia. In 538 BC Cyrus replaced Darius when he was deceased, and dating in scripture reflects this change (Weathers).

WEEK 38 READINGS

Day 1
Daniel 10-11
> Daniel's vision: 534 BC

Daniel 11: The first phrase of chapter eleven continues the quote from Michael, the heavenly messenger (10:21). Some of the most precise prophecies in the entire Bible are found in chapter eleven of Daniel, which contains prophecies of Alexander the Great, the Maccabees, and the Great Tribulation. The first 35 verses contain approximately 135 prophetic statements, now fulfilled (Rydelnick; Walvoord; Weathers).

Day 2
Daniel 12
> Daniel's last prophecy: 534 BC
Ezra 3
Psalms 106, 107

Daniel 12: 1290 days (v. 11) is 30 more than the three and a half years from the middle of the tribulation. This may allow time for the judgment of the nations (Matthew 25:31-46). Waiting 45 extra days (total of 1335 days) gives time for establishment of the Messianic government (Rydelnick).

Day 3
Ezra 4: 526-520 BC
Haggai 1-2
> Haggai's prophecy: 520 BC

Haggai 2: God called Governor Zerubbabel His signet ring (v. 23) and chose him as the Davidic ruler. This royal authority replaced the last of Judah's wicked kings (Jeremiah 22:24-27), Jehoiakim, Jehoiachin and Zedekiah. Zerubbabel is listed in the line for the Messiah (Luke 3:27) (NIV).

Day 4
Zechariah 1-6
 Zechariah's early prophecy: c. 520 BC

Day 5
Ezra 5: 520 BC
Zechariah 7-8: 518 BC
Psalm 130

Day 6
Ezra 6
 Rebuilding the temple, completion: 516 BC
Psalm 126
Esther 1
 Ahasuerus' banquet and Vashti's disposal: 483 BC
Zechariah 9
 Zechariah's later prophecy: c. 480 BC

Zechariah 9: Tyre (vs. 3-4) was a fortified commercial and naval power. About 160 years after this prophecy, Alexander the Great dismantled the city in seven months, but when he came to Jerusalem he did not destroy it (v. 8). Josephus recorded the story of the high priest, Jaddua, who met Alexander the Great as he advanced to Jerusalem, and showed the prophecies about him in the book of Daniel (8:5-8). Alexander entered peacefully and worshiped at the temple (Sandy; McGee).

Day 7
Zechariah 10-14

WEEK 39 READINGS

Day 1
Esther 2
     Esther crowned: 479 BC
Esther 3-4
     Haman's plan: 474 BC

Week 39: The times of this week's readings are the beginnings of the Golden Age of Greek art (477-431 BC) and philosophy. Socrates (470 - c. 399 BC) instructed Plato (428/7-348/7 BC), who instructed Aristotle (384-322 BC), who began tutorship in 338 BC of Alexander the Great (356-323 BC) (HCSB; Britannica.com; Biography.com).

Esther 3: Haman the Agagite (v. 1) was a descendant of King Agag of the Amalekites (1 Samuel 15:3, 20), whom Saul spared. Agag was put to death, but his family survived (Anderson).

Day 2
Esther 5-8

Day 3
Esther 9-10
     Feast of Purim established: 473 BC
Malachi 1-2
     Malachi's prophecy: c. 460 BC

Malachi was the last prophet in Old Testament times. He addressed social and religious problems similar to those in Ezra and Nehemiah. Malachi would have prophesied shortly before Ezra's return to Judah with revival in 458 BC, or before Nehemiah's second term as governor c. 435 BC. Linguists prefer the earlier date (Clendenen).

Malachi 1: God's statement "I hated Esau" (v. 3) reflected Esau's spiritual disinterest as compared to Jacob's continual desire for God's presence. Esau and his descendants, the Edomites, were known for their rebellion, violence, treachery, greed and pride (Jeremiah 49:7-22; Amos 1:9-12; Obadiah). God's holiness required complete destruction (Clendenen; NIV).

Day 4
Malachi 3-4
Ezra 7
    Ezra sent with temple gold: 458 BC
Psalm 119:1-32

Day 5
Psalm 119:33-176

Psalm 119: Here is confidence: God's word gives a sense of value (v. 37), freedom (v. 45), life (v. 93), wisdom (v. 98), safety (v. 101), direction (v. 105), joy (v. 111), hope (v. 114), understanding (v. 130), delight (v. 143), and peace (v. 165).

Day 6
Ezra 8-10

Day 7
Nehemiah 1-2
Nehemiah 4: 445 BC

Nehemiah 2: Artaxerxes had stopped the reconstruction in Jerusalem at an earlier date (Ezra 4:23). He was king of Persia (465-425 BC), the son of Xerxes (Ahasuerus), and stepson of Esther who became queen of Persia about 60 years after the first return of exiles to Jerusalem. She may have been influential for years after Xerxes' death. Persian kings were generous at feasts when Nehemiah made his request. Persian rulers prepared expensive tombs for ancestors, so Nehemiah's concern about his ancestors' burial place was taken seriously. Artaxerxes granted Nehemiah's requests and provided needed resources (vs. 6-8) (Halley; Anderson).

Nehemiah 4: Nehemiah hurried to rebuild the walls and did not have time to quarry new stones. They used "burnt stones" (v. 2) and all of the rubble from the destruction of Jerusalem in 586 BC when Nebuchadnezzar took the people of Judah into captivity.

WEEK 40 READINGS

Day 1
Nehemiah 5-6
Nehemiah 3

Jerusalem wall completed: 445 BC

Nehemiah 3: Scholars call chapter three the official record of gate construction and indicate it should be placed after chapter six which says the doors of the gates had not been installed. Placement of the doors finalized the construction (Anderson).

Day 2
Nehemiah 7-8
Psalm 147

Nehemiah 7: Not all people in the community were descendants of Abraham (v. 61). Some were Egyptians who departed with the Israelites in the Exodus, and some were captives from victorious battles who became servants. Genealogies were very important. Much was dependent on the tribe to which people belonged. Those from the tribe of Levi were able to resume temple service after captivity (v. 64) (Anderson).

Nehemiah 8: Ezra read from the Law to an attentive audience for several hours (v. 3) each day of this weeklong festival (v. 18). The law may have been read paragraph by paragraph in Hebrew, translated to, and explained (v. 8) in Aramaic, the language learned in captivity, and the language of Jesus' time (Anderson).

Day 3
Nehemiah 9-10

Nehemiah 10: Levites were not included in the land distribution when the Israelites came from Egypt, but the law provided for them with the people's tithes (vs. 37-38).

Day 4
Nehemiah 11-12: 432 BC

Day 5
Nehemiah 13
Psalm 115
1 Chronicles 1
    Genealogy recorded after exile: 430 BC

1 Chronicles 1: The genealogy from Adam's time to that of the return of exiles is in the next several chapters. Scholars believe Ezra may have written the Chronicles. Second Chronicles ends like the book of Ezra begins, and Ezra (or the writing scribe) would have had access to the historical records of the Chronicles. Edom's kings (vs. 43-51) may have lived during the times of the judges; otherwise the Chronicles focused on the kings of Judah (the southern kingdom) and covered the same time period as the books of the Kings. The line of the kings of Judah (chapter three) includes those in line for kingship after exile, and ends at a time when Ezra might have been the writer (Corduan).

Day 6
1 Chronicles 2-4

Day 7
1 Chronicles 5-6

1 Chronicles 6: Genealogies sometimes skip links, such as that of the Israelites when they were in Egypt. Also, Eli and his wicked sons Hophni and Phinehas at the time of Samuel's youth (1 Samuel 3:1) are not included in the genealogy (Corduan).

Week 41 Readings

Day 1
1 Chronicles 7-9

Time between the Old and New Testaments: After Persia captured Babylonia, Israelites turned from idolatry but became legalistic. The daily language was Aramaic with Hebrew in the synagogues. Persia was conquered by Alexander the Great in 333 BC. Ten years later his Greek world empire was divided among four generals, one of which annexed Judea to Egypt. Then Syria attacked Egypt, and Judea was a battleground between the two powers. About a hundred fifty years later Antiochus Epiphanes stopped Jewish sacrifices and put Greek idols in the temple. Mattathias, the Judean priest, revolted, and the Maccabean period began. The Romans began minting coins in 269 BC, took Jerusalem in 63 BC, and appointed Herod king of Judea, who slew the last of the Maccabees. Caesar Augustus became emperor of Rome in 19 BC. Jews lived in a Greek culture under Roman rule with Orientals nearby (McGee; Weathers).

Day 2
Luke 1
　　　　Gabriel's appearances: 5 BC
　　　　See Appendix G
Matthew 1: 5 BC

Matthew 1: Jesus' birth is listed as 4-5 BC. In AD 526 the Roman emperor asked a monk to make a calendar, reckon time around the birth of Christ, and arrange it relative to Rome's founding. The mistake was discovered many years later (Halley).

Day 3
Luke 2
>Birth and youth of Jesus: 5 BC – AD 7

Matthew 2
>Visit of the Magi: 4 BC

Matthew 3
>Baptism of Jesus: AD 29

Matthew 2: Magi was the name of a Medes and Persian tribe, and Daniel was chief over this priestly group of court officials called magicians (Daniel 4:9). This term referred to scholarship, not magic, and Daniel may have taught that the Messiah King would come. The Magi were called king makers and may have come on steeds, not camels. There may have been scores of wise men to be safe traveling through the desert with its bandits, and to cause such turmoil in Jerusalem (McGee; MacArthur; Halley; Clendenen; Walvoord).

Matthew 2: King Herod the Great was a maniac, and his fear and anger meant bloodshed. Jeremiah's "weeping in Ramah" (32:15) suggests the area of Herod's annihilation. Ramah was about as far north of Jerusalem as Bethlehem is south. The radius of this circle is ten to twelve miles (MacArthur; Clendenen).

Day 4
Luke 3
John 1-2: Beginning of time – AD 29

Day 5
Mark 1
Matthew 4
>Temptation of Jesus: AD 29

John 3

Day 6
Luke 4
John 4

Day 7
Luke 5
Mark 2
John 5

John 5: Legal matters required two witnesses. Jesus' witnesses were His work (and miracles) (v. 36), and the Old Testament (v. 39). Attacks on the Old Testament are attacks on Jesus (McGee).

WEEK 42 READINGS

Day 1
Luke 6
> Selection of disciples

Mark 3

Day 2
Matthew 5-7
> Sermon on the Mount

Matthew 5-7: The Sermon on the Mount expresses the mind of Christ, and is the platform of the Prince of Peace for when He establishes His kingdom on earth during the millennium. The law of the kingdom will then be enforced! The gospel is not included in the Sermon on the Mount, but this message convicts one of sin, and its commands can be followed only through the power of the Holy Spirit. After the Sermon on the Mount, Jesus performed miracles to demonstrate that while He gave the life principles, He also had the power to achieve them. Matthew regarded Jesus' life and teaching as illustrations of His sermon (McGee; Halley).

Day 3
Luke 7
Matthew 11

Luke 7: John's question (vs. 18-20) was one of confusion, not doubt. He saw Jesus doing the works of the promised Messiah as prophesied in Isaiah, but not anything political to overturn the Roman government and become the king of Israel. John was disappointed that a baptism of fire and judgment had not yet taken place (Matthew 3:11-12), and Jesus had not freed him from prison (Isaiah 61:1). Contrary to becoming a king, Jesus stated that His mission was to suffer, be rejected, killed and raised (Luke 9:22) (Luter; Quarles).

Matthew 11: "We played the flute for you, but you didn't dance" (v. 17) was an ancient version of the Simple Simon game. The people were likened to spoiled children that whined when they didn't get their way, and their friends did not respond appropriately. Israel's leaders did not respond to John or Jesus, but opposed them and their messages (vs. 18-19) (Quarles; NIV).

Day 4
Matthew 12
Mark 4
    The storm calmed

Matthew 12: The power Jesus had to cast out demons proved the Kingdom of God could overthrow Satan's kingdom. Jesus was the one to tie up the strong man (Satan) so He could rob his house (Hell) (v. 29), and claim Satan's desired captives for His own kingdom (Quarles).

Matthew 12: The strongest family relationship is between Christ and a believer—closer than that with an unsaved family member (vs. 46-50). Jesus' family did not believe in Him as the Messiah (Mark 3:21; John 7:5) until after His resurrection (McGee).

Day 5
Matthew 8
Mark 5

Mark 5: The people, and even Jesus' disciples, did not fully recognize Him as the Son of God (4:41), but the demons knew who He was (5:7). Demon possession led to self-destruction in both the man before he was healed, and in the pigs (Quarles; McLaren).

Day 6
Matthew 13
      Parable of the soils
Luke 8

Day 7
Matthew 9-10

WEEK **43** READINGS

Day 1
Matthew 14
> Feeding of 5000: AD 32
Mark 6

Mark 6: While the disciples focused on what they didn't have (v. 36), Jesus focused on what they did have (v. 38). Then when He walked on water, Jesus identified Himself as "I AM," God's divine name as given to Moses (Exodus 3:14). Jesus did what God alone could do (McLaren).

Day 2
John 6
Mark 7

Day 3
Matthew 15-16
> Jesus' death predicted
Mark 8

Matthew 15: In the hand washing ritual, water was poured over the fingers, first pointing up, then down, with more washing in between courses. Process, not cleanliness, was sacred since everything needed to be done in exact order, but the water did not need to be clean (Quarles).

Day 4
Matthew 17
> Transfiguration
Mark 9

Matthew 17: Jesus said some standing here would not die until they saw Him in His kingdom (16:28). One view is that this prophecy was fulfilled six days later at the transfiguration when three disciples saw Jesus, Moses, and Elijah, and witnessed the testimony from heaven that Jesus was the One to whom Old Testament prophecies pointed (Malachi 4:5-6). Peter's mistake was in treating Jesus and the prophets as equals. God's voice made the superiority and deity of Jesus certain (2 Peter 1:16-18). The presence of Moses representing the law, and Elijah the prophets, confirmed that all conditions for the coming of the Messiah had been met. They spoke of His coming death (Luke 9:31). All three had unusual deaths (Halley; Quarles; McGee).

Day 5
Matthew 18
Luke 9

Matthew 18: When Peter asked about forgiveness (v. 21), perhaps he knew seven was God's number of completeness. Some of God's perfect seven were the days of creation, the seven pairs of clean animals on the ark, Joshua's marches around Jericho, and Naaman dipping seven times in the Jordan. Jesus said forgiveness must be complete and unlimited, and told the story of forgiving an enormous debt of 10,000 talents. Yet the servant could not forgive what was trivial. Man thinks of measurable law, but God's terms are in immeasurable grace (Quarles; McGee).

Day 6
John 7-8

John 7: The temple police were Levites who kept order at the temple. They arrested criminals, but these police were unable to arrest Jesus after they heard His teaching (vs. 45-47; Matthew 7:28-29) (Yarbrough).

Day 7
Luke 10-11

WEEK 44 READINGS

Day 1
Luke 12-13

Luke 12: Some people are afraid they have committed the unforgiveable sin (v.10). The Holy Spirit convicts of sin and it is the rejection of Christ, which is unpardoned. But Christ died for all; all who repent and believe in Jesus will be forgiven (McGee).

Luke 13: The first/last dichotomy (v. 30) can be a mystery. The Jews were first in God's plan, but they rejected Christ, and will be the last to receive Him *en masse* near the end of the age. Gentiles were the last to receive news of the Creator God, and the first to believe in Jesus in large numbers (Romans 11:25-27). In Jesus' story of the vineyard workers, the last received the same pay as those who worked all day (Matthew 20:16). Those believing in Jesus at the end of their days will have eternal life (Luter; NIV).

Day 2
John 9-10
Luke 14

Luke 14: Jesus spoke of the banquet excuses (v. 18) as coming from religious leaders who would not believe Him. The highway/byway people who came were the Gentiles (Luter).

Day 3
Luke 15-17
Parables: Lost sheep, coin, son

Day 4
John 11
   Lazarus raised
Luke 18

Luke 18: The blind man confessed Jesus as Messiah when he called Him the Son of David (v. 38), but did the disciples understand? After Palm Sunday with peoples' cries proclaiming royalty, Peter called Jesus "Rabbi" (Mark 11:21). Rabbi simply meant master or teacher. Anyone who studied the Torah and Jewish Law could assume the title of Rabbi. Passion Week actions do not prove the disciples saw Him as deity (Luter; White, Jr.).

Day 5
Mark 10
Matthew 19

Day 6
Matthew 20
Luke 19
   Zacchaeus
John 12
   Triumphal Entry into Jerusalem: AD 33

John 12: If people are not coming to Christ to be saved, it is because He is not lifted up. Sinners don't see Jesus as Savior unless they see His death on the cross (vs. 32-33). Jesus came to save, not to judge. In the end, people will be judged by the word of God (vs. 47-48) (McGee).

Day 7
Mark 11
Matthew 21

Mark 11: Jesus presented Himself as King when He rode the animal that kings rode in times of peace. Robes and leafy branches were traditionally draped across the road to receive a king (2 Kings 9:13) (Kostenberger).

Week **45** Readings

Day 1
Luke 20
Matthew 22

Luke 20: Religious leaders tried hard to catch Jesus with trick questions, and Jesus asked His own difficult question, "How can they say that the Messiah is the son of David" (v. 41) and the Lord of David (v. 44)? He did not answer the question, that He was fully God (Lord) and fully human (son of David) (Luter).

Matthew 22: True faith provides the robe of righteousness, the "wedding garment" (v. 11 KJV). The absence of a robe identifies the wearer as a false disciple (Matthew 7:15-23) who wants to do his own thing and cannot give a true answer at the judgment seat (Quarles; McGee).

Day 2
Mark 12
Matthew 23

Day 3
Mark 13
Matthew 24

Mark 13: Roman armies leveled the temple and the city in AD 70. Archaeologists found "massive stones" (v. 1) surrounding the temple complex that were 42 feet long, 11 feet high, 14 feet deep and weighing over a million pounds (Luter; McLaren).

Day 4
Matthew 25
Luke 21
John 13
   The Last supper

John 13: Because so much travel was done walking in sandals on dusty roads, foot washing was a tradition. At times in the Old Testament, each person took care of this (Genesis 18:4; Judges 19:21). In Jesus' time, the lowest non-Jewish slaves were relegated to washing the feet of guests upon arrival, not during a meal (vs. 4-5). Jesus' humility (coming as a servant/ slave), is proclaimed in Philippians 2:5-8 (Kostenberger).

Day 5
John 14-16

John 15: The vine was a picture of Israel (Isaiah 5:1-7). This talk may have been given at the temple gates at Passover in full moonlight! The gates with vine engravings were always open. Jesus indicated it was not important to be identified with a religion, but to be in Him. The Greek word for prune also means clean. Without garden sprays, they washed, or poured water on the vines to remove bugs. Believers are clean through the washing of water through the word (Ephesians 5:26) (McGee).

John 15: Disciples in Bible times chose a rabbi to follow. Jesus changed the custom and chose His own disciples (v. 16), but they still needed to choose to follow Him (Kostenberger).

Day 6
John 17
Matthew 26

Day 7
Mark 14
John 18

WEEK 46 READINGS

Day 1
Luke 22
Mark 15
  Crucifixion: AD 33

Luke 22: Jesus' trial was illegal in procedures. Jewish trials were not to be held on the morning of a feast day; no formal defense was given for Jesus; and capital offenses required two days for the verdict to be reached (Luter).

Day 2
Matthew 27
Luke 23

Matthew 27: Roman law counted the refusal to defend oneself as an admission of guilt (v. 14) (Quarles).

Matthew 27: 20-26: Early literature indicated that Barabbas' full name was Jesus Bar Abbas, which could mean he was the son of a famous teacher, or son of Rabba. If that is true, Pilate gave the Jews a choice to release Jesus, the son of a teacher, or Jesus, the Son of God. Another view is that Barabbas meant son of the father, so the choice was between him and Jesus, the true Son of the Father (Quarles; McLaren).

Luke 23: Jesus died at the time of afternoon sacrifices (vs. 44-46). Priests would have been present to observe the tearing of the curtain, the barrier between man and God (Quarles).

Day 3
John 19-20
   Resurrection

John 19: The sign on the cross (v. 20) was written in Aramaic for the religious Hebrew Jews, in Latin for the Roman government of law and order, and in Greek for their culture and foreign visitors (McGee; NIV).

John 19: When a soldier thrust a spear in Jesus' side, out came blood and water (v. 34). Medical authorities have said that when the heart ruptures, blood collects in the lining and becomes a watery/bloody mixture. It may be said that as Christ bore the sin of the world He died of a broken heart (Halley).

Day 4
Matthew 28
Mark 16
John 21
Luke 24

Day 5
Acts 1-3
   Ascension and Pentecost: AD 33

Acts 1-2: The cloud (1:9) wind (2:2) and fire (2:3) represented God's presence. God's cloud led the Israelites in wilderness wandering (Exodus 13:21), filled the temple (1 Kings 8:10-11), took Jesus from earth (Acts 1:9), and Jesus will return in a cloud (Mark 14:62). Wind was sometimes associated with judgment (Jeremiah 30:23; Hosea 8:7; Jonah 1:4; 4:8), but was present at the Holy Spirit's coming (Acts 2:2). Fire represented the Holy Spirit to purify and lead. Moses saw fire in the bush, in the pillar at night for Israelites in the wilderness, and at Mt. Sinai when the commandments were given (Exodus 3:2; 13:21; 19:18). In the New Testament the tongues of fire (Acts 2:3-4) represented speech and the communication of the gospel (Porter; Register).

Day 6
Acts 4-6

Day 7
Acts 7-8
    Stephen martyred
    Phillip and the Ethiopian eunuch

WEEK **47** READINGS

Day 1
Acts 9
> Saul on Damascus road: AD 34
Acts 10
> Peter's vision: AD 40

Acts 9: With murder in his heart, Saul pulled Christians out of the synagogue (vs. 1-2), the meeting hall that could be started with ten men who gathered for prayer and the reading of the law. As Christians scattered, they built synagogues; many have been found in Palestine and in neighboring lands (White, Jr.).

Day 2
Acts 11-13
> Peter's prison escape: AD 44
> Paul's first missionary journey: AD 47-49

Acts 12: Jewish beliefs included guardian angels that sometimes appeared after a person died. It was easy for the prayer group (v.12) to believe this was Peter's angel after execution (Porter).

Day 3
Acts 14-15
> Jerusalem Council: AD 49
Galatians 1
> Galatians written: AD 49

Acts 14-15: The churches planted by Paul and Barnabas in their first missionary journey were in Galatia, a Roman province (13:14 - 14:23). Believing Jews were confused: could uncircumcised Gentiles be saved? The Jerusalem Council (15:5-20) considered this question. Peter's testimony of seeing Gentiles saved showed that conversion was the same for all people. The restrictions given to new Gentile Christians (15:20) may have helped them stop activities that were part of pagan temple practices (Porter).

Day 4
Galatians 2-4

Galatians 4: The fullness of time (v. 4) for Christ's coming was during 'general worldwide peace under the Romans. Basically one language was spoken, and excellent roads were in place in the empire. It was the time of cruel deaths on the cross, fulfilling prophecy. Jesus' death was not a stoning, and this was before the coliseum lions. The law claimed, "anyone hung on a tree is under God's curse" (Deuteronomy 21:23; Galatians 3:13) (Luter).

Day 5
Galatians 5-6
Acts 16
      Paul's second missionary journey: AD 49-52
James 1
      James written: c. AD 48-52

Day 6
James 2-5

James 1-3: God tests faith in various ways: with trials and suffering (1:2-12); not with evil, although He permits it (1:13-14). His word (1:22-27) as well as attitudes, actions (2:1-13), and works (2:14-26) are tests of faith. John Calvin said, "Faith alone saves. But faith that saves is not alone." God also tests faith by the tongue (chapter 3). The heart is the storehouse of the tongue, which displays one's character (McGee).

Day 7
Acts 17
Paul at Mars Hill: AD 50
1 Thessalonians 1-4
1 Thessalonians written: AD 51

1 Thessalonians 3: In Athens, after Paul left Thessalonica, (Acts 17:5-16), he wondered how the Thessalonians were doing (3:5), and Timothy brought a good report (Davis).

WEEK **48** READINGS

Day 1
1 Thessalonians 5
2 Thessalonians 1-3
>2 Thessalonians written: AD 51
Acts 18
>Priscilla and Aquila: AD 53

Day 2
Acts 19
>Paul's third missionary journey: AD 53-57
1 Corinthians 1-2
>1 Corinthians written: AD 56

Day 3
1 Corinthians 3-6

1 Corinthians 4: Paul mentioned being a spectacle for the world to see, "like men condemned to die" (v. 9). This exposure was God's doing, to display the apostles before the world. Spectacle comes from a word meaning theatrical display, and refers to a parade of criminals after a military victory. Captives at the front were set free, but captives at the end were the last show in the arena, and this was their execution (Tomlinson).

1 Corinthians 6: About being one with the Lord and one with Him in spirit (v.17), Pastor Steve Abbott said, "United with Christ, we are one with Him in spirit. Everything we do involves Christ. Everything!"

Day 4
1 Corinthians 7-10

Day 5
1 Corinthians 11-14

1 Corinthians 13: Love is the greatest (v. 13) and it will continue forever. In eternity faith will be achieved, and everything for which one hopes will be completed (Tomlinson).

1 Corinthians 14: Evidently there was an unusual display of the popular gift of speaking in foreign languages (vs. 1-40). Few apostles met the churches that were far apart. Communication and transportation were slow. Written records were almost non-existent, and false claims abundant. Everybody wanted the gift of tongues and the prestige associated with it (Halley).

Day 6
1 Corinthians 15-16
2 Corinthians 1
  2 Corinthians written: AD 56

2 Corinthians 1: First Corinthians was not well received. False apostles had troubled the church (2 Corinthians 11:13-15) as reported by Timothy (1 Corinthians 4:17; 16:10-11). While Paul was at Ephesus, he took time to visit Corinth again (13:2). He then sent a letter of rebuke by Titus who reported that many in the church had repented. That letter has been lost. Paul wrote this letter and promised to come again (Acts 20:3) (Easley).

Day 7
2 Corinthians 2-5

2 Corinthians 2: After military victories, the Roman army would parade through Rome. Pagan temples burned incense, and fragrance would waft over the city. Paul said that Christ gave His fragrance (v. 15) to us for a pleasing aroma to God as we spread the knowledge of Him (vs. 14-16) (Fisher; Ochoa; McGee).

WEEK **49** READINGS

Day 1
2 Corinthians 6-9

Day 2
2 Corinthians 10-12

2 Corinthians 12: Paul's vision of the third heaven (12:2) would have been in AD 42, or a real experience might have been at the Lystra stoning (Acts 14:19) (Easley).

Day 3
2 Corinthians 13
Acts 20
> End of Paul's third journey
Romans 1
> Romans written: AD 57

Romans 1: Paul spent almost a year in Greece (Acts 20:1-5), and Romans was written in Corinth. He may not have visited Rome before he wrote this letter. Some Romans may have heard the gospel when they visited Jerusalem at Pentecost (Acts 2:10). Paul led Aquila and Priscilla and others to Christ who later moved to the capital city (Acts 18:1-2; Romans 16:3) (Halley; Blum).

Day 4
Romans 2-5

Romans 3: Three ways of describing what Jesus did on the cross are named (vs. 24-25). The slave market gave the term of <u>redemption</u> when one purchased freedom for a slave—he was redeemed. The courts gave the term of <u>justification</u> when the judge declared justified (not guilty) one who was condemned. <u>Propitiation</u> is the removal of God's punishment for sin by Jesus' sacrifice. It was a term of the sacrificial system from the Day of Atonement at the temple. An animal received God's wrath at the sacrifice. A scapegoat, laden with men's sins was sent outside the camp. God's wrath over sin was put on Jesus on the cross, outside the city. Yet for His unfathomable love, He declared believers not guilty (Blum; Feinberg; NIV).

Day 5
Romans 6-8

Romans 8: God calls the predestined (vs. 29-30) to be conformed (patterned) to resemble His Son. The predestined ones He called are the whosoever wills, and those not called are the whosoever won'ts. It is still always man's choice (McGee).

Day 6
Romans 9-11

Romans 9-11: This passage has puzzled many scholars. K. H. Rengstorff of Germany in 1949 said, "During the years of its sufferings, the Confessing Church learnt that Romans 9-11 held the key to the understanding of the New Testament." Paul wrote about God's sovereignty (9), about responsibility of humans (10), and about God's final purpose (11). There were questions such as, wasn't the Messiah supposed to excel King David's glory? Wasn't He to deliver Israel from Gentiles and be the supreme ruler? Israel had not been delivered, and if Jesus was Messiah, but didn't accomplish what was expected, were God's promises trustworthy? These chapters answer tough questions about how Jesus could be the Messiah and yet be rejected by Israel (Blum).

Day 7
Romans 12-15

Week 50 Readings

Day 1
Romans 16
Acts 21-22
Paul leaving Ephesus; Jerusalem riot: AD 57

Day 2
Acts 23-25
Paul's defense to Felix, Festus: AD 59

Day 3
Acts 26-27
Paul before King Agrippa
Paul's shipwreck: AD 59

Acts 26: Herod Agrippa ll, the last of the Herodian kings, began to rule in AD 52. His father, Herod Agrippa l killed James (Acts 12:2). His grandfather, Herod Antipas killed John the Baptist (Matthew 14:10). His great grandfather murdered the children of Bethlehem (Matthew 2:16) (Halley; Porter).

Day 4
Acts 28
Philemon 1
Philemon written: AD 61
Colossians 1-2
Colossians written: AD 61

Acts 28: Paul wanted to visit the church at Rome (Romans 15:32) but not this way! While he was in house arrest, Paul taught and mentored many (v. 30). There is not record of an actual trial.

Philemon 1: The church in Colosse met in Philemon's house (churches were not housed in buildings until the third century). Paul was expecting freedom (v. 22), and may have been released, then arrested again later (Harris).

Colossians 1: The Colossians were mostly Gentiles from Phrygia and Greece (Acts 2:10). Epaphras had established the church in Colosse (v. 7). At this time he may have been in prison with Paul (Philemon 23) and told him about the false teachers in Colosse.

Colossians 2: Paul wrote this letter to counter the heresy or philosophy (v. 8), which seemed to be a mixture of Jewish, Greek and Oriental religions. The heresy included worshiping angels (mediators between man and God); asceticism (the extreme denial of self) (vs. 21-22); and some Jewish requirements (Kostenberger; Halley).

Day 5
Colossians 3-4
Ephesians 1-2
 Ephesians written: AD 61

Ephesians 2: Paul spent about three years in Ephesus (present day Turkey) (Acts 19). Later while in prison in Rome, he heard there was much division between Jews and Gentiles in the area. Paul's emphasis in writing to the Ephesians was unity of the church in Christ through the power of the Spirit. The Head (Christ) and the body (believers) are one regardless of ethnic differences (vs. 11-22) (Dockery).

Day 6
Ephesians 3-6

Day 7
Philippians 1-4

    Philippians written: AD 62

Philippians 1: Paul planted a church in Philippi, the capital city in the Macedonian Roman Colony about AD 51. Initial difficulties (Acts 16:16-24) put Paul and Silas in jail where the jailor asked how to be saved. Now in prison again, Paul witnessed to the Roman soldiers who guarded him (vs. 12-14), and his message reached some of the civil service members that made up Caesar's household (4:22) (Melick, Jr.).

WEEK 51 READINGS

Day 1
1 Timothy 1-6
> 1 Timothy written: c. AD 62-64

1, II Timothy and Titus: These books were written to coworkers, and give insights into church government. They teach the importance of right doctrine and proper behavior (Van Neste).

Day 2
1 Peter 1-5

1 Peter 1-2: This letter written AD 64 was to churches founded by Paul in the Roman provinces (modern Turkey). Nero was persecuting Christians, and Peter reminded them of their original state without Christ (1:14,18). Now as God's people, they were temporary residents and strangers (2:9-11), but their ultimate home was heaven (Halley; Wilder).

Day 3
Titus 1-3
> Titus written: c. AD 62-64
Jude 1
> Jude written: c. AD 66
2 Peter 1
> 2 Peter written: c. AD 66

Jude 1: A half-brother of Jesus, Jude believed in Him after the resurrection. Jude heard of false teachers sneaking heresy into churches and warned about three examples of the apostates (v. 11). Cain hated the righteous and wanted a bloodless gospel. Balaam, good with words, corrupted the gospel for personal gain. Korah tried to prohibit the gospel by rebellion. Jude called for a faith with solid doctrine (Rogers; Wilder).

2 Peter 1: Peter was imprisoned, and knew he would be martyred (v. 14) by Nero who reigned from AD 54-68. Peter and Jude were concerned about false teachers and gave examples of those judged for hatred, greed, and rebellion (Wilder).

Day 4
2 Peter 2-3
2 Timothy 1-2
>2 Timothy written: between AD 65 and 67

Day 5
2 Timothy 3-4
Hebrews 1-4
>Hebrews written: between AD 64 and AD 68

Hebrews: Who wrote Hebrews? is an old question. Suggestions are Paul, Luke, Clement of Rome, Barnabas, Apollos, Timothy, Peter, Silas, Phillip, Priscilla, Jude and Aristion. Paul indicated he had received the gospel directly from the Lord (1 Corinthians 15:8, Galatians 1:12); the writer of Hebrews states that he received the gospel from others who knew Jesus (2:3). Paul called Timothy his son in the faith (1 Timothy 1:2); in Hebrews Timothy is called our brother (13:23). The writer mentioned persecution (10:32-34), which dates to Nero's time. Hebrews was written in flawless beautiful Greek (Yarnell III; NIV).

Day 6
Hebrews 5-9

Hebrews 6: Dr. J. Vernon McGee explained how salvation is not by works, salvation is immutable – not lost if one commits major sin and "falls away" (v. 6). One who falls cannot be brought back for a good testimony, and to continue good works for God. Peter fell. John Mark failed. The same word is used for Jesus' fall to pray in the garden. This section of Hebrews

6 does not deal with salvation, but with rewards. Works will be tested by fire and burned (v. 8) if they are wood, hay, and stubble. Works are the fruit of salvation, not the root of salvation (v. 9) (McGee).

Day 7
Hebrews 10-12

Week 52 Readings

Day 1
Hebrews 13
1 John 1-3
    1, 2 and 3 John written: AD 80s

1, 2, 3 John: According to writers in the second century, John left Jerusalem after the Romans destroyed the temple and the city. He was a leader in the church of Ephesus, the city from which he most likely wrote these letters. He noted the problem of false teachers in the church, and his main themes were guarding and walking in the truth, which involves obedience, loving others; and being certain of eternal life and the forgiveness of sins (Yarbrough).

Day 2
1 John 4-5
2 John 1
3 John 1
Revelation 1
    Revelation written: c. AD 95

Revelation: Scholars have various dates for the writing of Revelation, but consensus brings it to the mid-90s. Persecution of Christians after Nero's time took place during Domitian's rule from AD 81-96. During this time John was exiled to the island of Patmos. The reference to five fallen kings (17:10) supports this date. Much of the book focuses on end times, but it also concentrates on practical choices and the consequences of resulting actions (Luter).

Day 3
Revelation 2-5

Revelation 3: Jesus told the Laodiceans that He wished they were either hot or cold, but not lukewarm (vs. 5-16). They recognized the metaphor because of their two sources of water. From Hierapolis hot spring water traveled about six miles to get to them. Cold refreshing water from the melting snow of Mount Cadmus came to Colosse, about twelve miles away from Laodicea. Travelers came from miles for the therapeutic hot pools of Hierapolis or the refreshing cold water of Colosse. By the time the water reached Laodicea, it was lukewarm, useless and disgusting. Jesus indicated the Laodiceans had not left the faith, but they were self-centered and their faith was lukewarm and useless just like their water (Linzey).

Day 4
Revelation 6-10

Day 5
Revelation 11-14

Day 6
Revelation 15-18

Day 7
Revelation 19-22

Congratulations for reading through the entire book of God's word! Blessings to you as you continue to spend time in God's word. Each reading can result in new insights of His truth, His light. "God is light and there is absolutely no darkness in Him" (1 John 1:5).

AUTHOR'S NOTE

I hope that you appreciated this guide and will recommend it to others. My goal is to encourage others to read God's word in its entirety. Each year it is my delight to read using this guide, and amazingly, I always find portions that seem new to me, or that bring new insight to the reading.

Books are often found by the reviews written about them. Thank you for giving a quick review on your bookseller's website.

APPENDIX A

Isaac and Jesus

The story of Isaac in Genesis 21-22 is similar in some ways to the events of the life of Jesus:

Both births were promised in prophecy.
Both were long awaited births.
Both were named before birth (Genesis 17:19, Luke 1:31).
Both were born at an appointed time (Genesis 21:12, Galatians 4:4).
Both births were miraculous, though of a different nature (one to an old barren woman, One to a young virgin).
Both mothers thought this was beyond belief (Genesis 18:10-12, Luke 1:34).
Each father gave his only son (Genesis 22:2, John 3:16).
Both may have been in their early 30's at the time of sacrifice.
Both were a particular joy to, and were loved by, their fathers.
Both went obediently to be sacrificed.
Both carried the wood for the sacrifice.
A ram was offered as a substitute for Isaac. Jesus, the Lamb of God was offered as a sacrifice for mankind.
Both sacrifices were offered on Mount Moriah.
God spared Isaac, but did not spare His own Son (Romans 8:32).
Both were saved from death (one before, and One after).
Both arrived back from the dead after three days (Abraham and Isaac's was a three-day journey).

The fathers sent servants to look for a bride: Abraham sent his servant to get a bride (Rebecca) for Isaac. The Father God sends evangelists to get a bride (the church) for Christ.

All nations will be blessed as the gospel goes to all (Genesis 22:18).

The servants' primary purpose was to tell about the riches of the father's house (Genesis 24:35, John 14:2).

We are joint heirs with God's Son, and Abraham's children.

Most ideas are from Dr. J. Vernon McGee.
Compiled by Jane Weathers.

APPENDIX B

Joseph and Jesus

The events in the life of Joseph in Genesis are similar in some ways to the events in the life of Jesus:

Joseph was a beloved son of his father - Genesis 37:3. Jesus was the beloved Son of His Father - Matthew 3:17; 17:5.
Both lives were recorded without mention of sin.
Both were truth speakers - Genesis 37:2; Hebrews 7:26; John 7:7.
Joseph was hated when he told his dreams and his brothers noted a coming dominion - Genesis 37:8. Jesus was hated when He told of coming dominion - Matthew 26:64.
Both were suffering servants.
There was conspiracy against both - Genesis 37:18; Matthew 26:3-4.
Both suffered abuse - Genesis 37:23-24; Matthew 37:23-24; 27:26-29.
Both were stripped of their robes - Genesis 37:23: Matthew 27:28, 35.
Both were arrested - Genesis 39:20: Matthew 26:50.
Both were sold for the price of a slave - Genesis 37:28; Matthew 26:15.
God was with both - Genesis 39:2.
Both gave credit to God - Genesis 41:16.
Both became an exalted sovereign - Genesis 41:38-44; 1 Peter 3:22.
Joseph was next in command to Pharaoh - Genesis 41:40. Jesus sat down at the right hand of God - Acts 2:33.
Joseph's name was revered. Jesus' name is above all names - Philippians 2:9-10.

People bowed before Joseph. Every knee will bow before Jesus - Philippians 2:10; Romans 14:11.

People cried to make way as they rode by - Genesis 41:43; Matthew 21:9.

Both made provision for seekers - Genesis 41:55-57.

Joseph was the only hope for his world - Genesis 41:49. Jesus is the only hope for today's world - Acts 4:12.

Joseph had plenty of supply without number - Genesis 41:49. Jesus gave out of His riches - Romans 9:23; 10:12; 11:33.

Both made themselves known - Genesis 45:3-4. Jesus must reveal Himself to you - Matthew 11:27.

Both wanted to save others with love and grace - Genesis 45:4-5.

Both forgave - Genesis 45:4-5.

Both gave the invitation - come to me - Genesis 45:4.

God sent both - Genesis 45:8; John 3:16.

Both could forgive and restore - Genesis 50:20.

Both commissioned brothers - go and tell - Genesis 45:9, 13; Matthew 28:19-20.

The brothers went out as evangelists as if to say, "He wants us to be with him" - Genesis 45:26-27; John 14:3.

Both prepared a place - Genesis 45:10; 47:11; John 14:2-3.

Both provided for the needs of his followers - Genesis 47:12.

Joseph told his brothers not to quarrel - Genesis 45:24. Jesus said to love others - John 13:34-35.

Ideas from Adrian Rogers' sermon, "Joseph, a Portrait of Jesus."
Compiled by Jane Weathers

APPENDIX C

Moses and Jesus

Moses, leader of the Israelites, said God would "raise up for you a prophet like me," and they "must listen to him" (Deuteronomy 18:15, Acts 7:37). The events in the life of Moses are similar in some ways to the events in the life of Jesus:

±Both Moses and Jesus were born during difficult times in national Jewish history.
*Pharaoh destroyed infant boys at the time of Moses' birth. King Herod destroyed infant boys at the time of Jesus' birth.
Baby Moses was saved from death while in Egypt. Baby Jesus was saved from death while in Egypt.
±Moses surrendered the riches of Egypt. Jesus willingly laid aside His glory.
±Moses was called the servant of God. Jesus was called the Son of God.
Both Moses and Jesus fasted for 40 days (Deuteronomy 9:9).
±Moses was the people's liaison with God. Jesus is the mediator between God and people (1 Timothy 2:5-6).
*Moses did miraculous signs and wonders as sent by the Lord (Deuteronomy 34:10-12). Jesus performed many miracles during His lifetime on earth.
Moses brought the Law from God to the people (Exodus 34:4, 29). Jesus came to fulfill the law (Matthew 5:17).
Moses was learned in all the wisdom of Egypt (Acts 7:22). Jesus was learned in all the wisdom of God (Luke 2:52).

±Moses' face was radiant after meeting with God (Exodus 34:29). Jesus' face shone like the sun on the Mount of Transfiguration (Matthew 17:2). Moses' countenance reflected God's glory. Jesus is the Lord of glory (John 11:4, Philippians 2:10-11, Hebrews 13:21).

Moses taught all of the Law (Leviticus 19 ff.). Jesus taught about the kingdoms of God (Matthew 6:33, Mark 10:14-15) and heaven (Matthew 13:11; 18:1-4).

The Israelites rebelled against Moses (Numbers 16:1-3, Hebrews 3:16). The Jews rejected Jesus (Matthew 21:42, Mark 8:31, Luke 17:25).

Moses' teachings are veiled to the unrepentant (2 Corinthians 3:15; 2 Timothy 3:8). Jesus' words are veiled to the unrepentant (2 Corinthians 4:3-4).

Moses was faithful as a prophet (Hebrews 3:5, Numbers 12:6-7). Jesus is faithful as our High Priest (Hebrews 3:2).

±Both Moses and Jesus outlined guidelines for worship, avoiding idolatry, and treatment of the less fortunate (Deuteronomy 12-16).

±Both Moses and Jesus expressed compassion for the people (Numbers 27:17; Matthew 9:36).

±Both Moses and Jesus made intercession for the people (Deuteronomy 9:18; Hebrews 7:25).

±Both Moses and Jesus spoke with God directly (Exodus 34:29).

±Both Moses and Jesus relayed to the people what God said (Numbers 11:18; John 12:49-50).

±Both Moses and Jesus were mediators of a covenant (Deuteronomy 29:1; Hebrews 8:6-7).

*Miriam and Aaron doubted Moses' leadership (Numbers 12). Jesus' family doubted Him (Mark 3:21).

The Israelites wanted to put Moses to death (Exodus 17:4, Numbers 14:10). The religious leaders wanted to put Jesus to death (Matthew 14:5; Matthew 21:46, John 11:8).

Moses was called humble (Numbers 12:3). Jesus was called meek (Philippians 2:8, Matthew 11:29; 21:5).

*Moses put a serpent up on a pole to save lives (John 3:14). Jesus was put up on a cross to save lives (John 3:14-18).

±Both Moses and Jesus finished the work God gave them to do.

Both Moses and Jesus will have songs sung about them (Revelation 15:3).

*Ideas from *Missions Mosaic*, "Prayer Patterns," August 2014.
± Ideas from Allen Tilley.
Other ideas from McGee.
Compiled by Jane Weathers

APPENDIX D

Psalm Correlations

The reference listed below precedes the Psalm to the left.

1	1 Chr 16	31	2 Sm 21	61	2 Sm 18	91	Deut 32	121	Isa 37
2	2 Sm 2	32	2 Sm 12	62	2 Sm 15	92	1 Chr 26	122	1 Chr 14
3	2 Sm 15	33	1 Chr 16	63	2 Sm 17	93	2 Chr 7	123	2 Chr 30
4	2 Sm 21	34	1 Sm 21	64	1 Sm 24	94	Isa 31	124	1 Sm 30
5	1 Chr 18	35	1 Sm 24	65	1 Chr 24	95	2 Chr 5	125	2 Chr 30
6	1 Sm 21	36	1 Sm 18	66	2 Chr 14	96	1 Chr 17	126	Ezra 6
7	1 Sm 24	37	1 Chr 29	67	2 Kgs 22	97	1 Chr 17	127	2 Chr 7
8	1 Chr 17	38	1 Chr 21	68	2 Sm 6	98	2 Sm 9	128	2 Chr 31
9	1 Chr 20	39	2 Sm 20	69	2 Sm 18	99	1 Kgs 2	129	Isa 37
10	1 Sm 30	40	2 Sm 3	70	1 Sm 20	100	1 Chr 16	130	Zech 8
11	1 Sm 21	41	2 Sm 17	71	2 Chr 17	101	1 Chr 17	131	2 Sm 3
12	1 Sm 19	42	Ezek 11	72	1 Kgs 2	102	Ezek 22	132	2 Chr 5
13	2 Sm 17	43	Ezek 11	73	1 Kgs 2	103	1 Sm 18	133	1 Sm 18
14	1 Sm 17	44	2 Chr 20	74	2 Kgs 25	104	2 Chr 3	134	2 Chr 31
15	1 Sm 17	45	1 Kgs 3	75	1 Chr 16	105	1 Chr 17	135	2 Chr 7
16	1 Chr 14	46	Isa 37	76	Isa 37	106	Ezra 3	136	2 Chr 7
17	1 Sm 19	47	Isa 37	77	Isa 36	107	Ezra 3	137	2 Kgs 24
18	2 Sm 22	48	2 Chr 20	78	1 Chr 21	108	1 Chr 14	138	1 Sm 16
19	1 Chr 16	49	1 Kgs 10	79	2 Kgs 25	109	1 Sm 25	139	2 Sm 21
20	1 Chr 19	50	2 Sm 22	80	2 Kgs 17	110	1 Chr 11	140	1 Sm 27
21	1 Chr 11	51	2 Sm 12	81	1 Chr 26	111	1 Kgs 17	141	1 Sm 27

22	1 Sm 29	52	1 Sm 22	82	Isa 31	112	1 Chr 17	142	1 Sm 24
23	1 Chr 18	53	1 Chr 20	83	2 Chr 20	113	1 Chr 17	143	1 Sm 19
24	1 Chr 17	54	1 Sm 26	84	2 Chr 7	114	Josh 3	144	2 Sm 21
25	1 Sm 23	55	2 Sm 15	85	Jer 34	115	Neh 12	145	1 Sm 18
26	2 Sm 15	56	1 Sm 21	86	1 Sm 20	116	Jonah 2	146	1 Chr 17
27	1 Sm 29	57	1 Sm 24	87	2 Chr 7	117	2 Kgs 11	147	Neh 8
28	1 Sm 21	58	1 Sm 29	88	1 Chr 21	118	1 Chr 29	148	2 Chr 4
29	2 Sm 21	59	1 Sm 19	89	1 Chr 21	119	Ezra 7	149	1 Kgs 2
30	1 Chr 28	60	1 Chr 18	90	Ex 34	120	Isa 36	150	1 Chr 17

Index to abbreviations:

Chr – Chronicles	Isa – Isaiah	Neh – Nehemiah
Deut – Deuteronomy	Jer – Jeremiah	Sm – Samuel
Ex – Exodus	Josh – Joshua	Zech – Zechariah
Ezek – Ezekiel	Kgs – Kings	

APPENDIX E

Kings of the Divided Kingdom

Listing the first year of the reign of each king (after David and Solomon) and length of reign in years unless otherwise noted. All dates are BC. Apparent time discrepancies may be due in part to overlapping reigns (co-regency), intervals of anarchy, and parts of years counted as years. Note that some kings were known by more than one name.

Judah (Southern Kingdom)	Israel (Northern Kingdom)
931 Rehoboam 17	931 Jeroboam 22
913 Abijah/Abijam 3	910 Nadab 2
911 Asa 41	909 Baasha 24
873 Jehoshaphat 25	886 Elah 2
853 Jehoram/Joram 8	885 Zimri 7 days
841 Ahaziah 1	885 Tibni
841 Athaliah 6	885 Omri 12
835 Joash 40	874 Ahab 22
796 Amaziah 29	853 Ahaziah 2
792 Uzziah/Azariah 52	852 Jehoram/Joram 12
750 Jotham 16	841 Jehu 27
735 Ahaz/Jehoahaz 16	814 Jehoahaz 17
716 Hezekiah 29	798 Jehoash/Joash 16
697 Manasseh 55	793 Jeroboam II 41
643 Amon 2	753 Zechariah 3 months

641 Josiah 31

609 Jehoaz/Jehoahaz 3 months

609 Jehoiakim/Eliakim 11

598 Jehoiachin/Jeconiah/ Coniah 3 months

597 Zedekiah/Mattaniah 11

(586) Judah taken captive by the Babylonians)

752 Shallum 1 month

752 Menahem 10

742 Pekahiah 2

740 Pekah 8

732 Hoshea 9

(722 Israel taken captive by the Assyrians)

APPENDIX F

Prophets and Kings

Dates for prophets and kings vary between scholars. The following timetable gives supposed dates of their ministry and reign. Kings listed may have reigned at the time of the prophet's ministry, whether or not they were involved with the prophet.

PROPHET	BC DATES	KINGS OF JUDAH	KINGS OF ISRAEL
Ahijah	934-909	Rehoboam, Abijah, Asa	Jeroboam, Nadab, Baasha
Elijah	870-845	Jehoshaphat, Jehoram	Ahab, Ahaziah, Jehoram
Micaiah	856	Jehoshaphat, Ahab	Ahab
Jehu	853	Jehoshaphat, Jehoram	Ahab, Ahaziah
Elisha	845-800	Jehoram, Ahaziah, Athaliah, Joash	Jehoram, Jehu, Jehoahaz
Jonah	781	Uzziah	Jeroboam II
Amos	765-754	Uzziah, Jotham?	Jeroboam II
Hosea	758-725	Uzziah, Jotham, Ahaz, Hezekiah	Jeroboam II, Zechariah Shallum, Menahem, Pekahiah, Pekah, Hoshea
Isaiah	740-698	Uzziah, Jotham, Ahaz, Hezekiah	Pekahiah, Pekah, Hoshea
Micah	738-698	Jotham, Ahaz, Hezekiah, Manasseh	Pekah, Hoshea
Oded	733	Ahaz	Pekah

Joel	between 722 and 605	Ahaz? Hezekiah? Manasseh? Amon? Josiah? Jehoaz? Jehoiakim?	
Nahum	658-615	Manasseh, Amon, Josiah	
Zephaniah	640-626	Josiah	
Jeremiah	627-580	Josiah, Jehoaz, Jehoiakim, Jehoiachin, Zedekiah	
Huldah	621	Josiah	
Habakkuk	608-598	Jehoiakim, Jehoiachin, Zedekiah	
Daniel	605-534	Jehoiakim, Jehoiahin, Zedekiah	
Ezekiel	593-570	Jehoiachin?, Zedekiah	
Obadiah	586	Zedekiah	
Zechariah	520-480		
Haggai	520		
Malachi	460		

APPENDIX G

The Chronology of the Gospels

#	SUBJECT	MATT.	MARK	LUKE	JOHN
1	Writing purpose			1:1-4	
2	God became human				1:1-18
3	Genealogy to Jesus	1:1-17		3:23-38	
4	Angel about birth of John			1:5-25	
5	Angel about birth of Jesus			1:26-38	
6	Mary's visit to Elizabeth			1:39-56	
7	Birth of John the Baptist			1:57-80	
8	Angel's visit to Joseph	1:18-25			
9	Jesus born in Bethlehem			2:1-7	
10	Shepherds visit Jesus			2:8-20	
11	Jesus presented in temple			2:21-38	
12	Visit of magi	2:1-12			
13	Escape to Egypt	2:13-18			
14	Return to Nazareth	2:19-23		2:39-40	
15	Jesus to religious leaders			2:41-52	
16	John prepares the way	3:1-12	1:1-8	3:1-18	
17	Jesus is baptized	3:13-17	1:9-11	3:21-22	
18	Jesus tempted by Satan	4:1-11	1:12-13	4:1-13	
19	John's mission				1:19-28
20	John says Jesus is Messiah				1:29-34
21	First disciples				1:35-51
22	Water to wine				2:1-11
23	Jesus clears the temple				2:12-25
24	Nicodemus' visit				3:1-21
25	John says more about Jesus				3:22-36
26	Herod imprisons John			3:19-20	

27	The woman at the well				4:1-26
28	The spiritual harvest				4:27-38
29	Samaritans believe Jesus				4:39-42
30	Jesus preaches in Galilee	4:12-17	1:14-15	4:14-15	4:43-45
31	Jesus heals official's son				4:46-54
32	Jesus rejected at Nazareth			4:16-30	
33	Fishermen follow Jesus	4:18-22	1:16-20		
34	Jesus teaches with authority		1:21-28	4:31-37	
35	Jesus heals many	8:14-17	1:29-34	4:38-41	
36	Jesus preaches in Galilee	4:23-25	1:35-39	4:42-44	
37	Miraculous catch of fish			5:1-11	
38	Jesus heals a leper	8:1-4	1:40-45	5:12-16	
39	Jesus heals paralyzed man	9:1-8	2:1-12	5:17-26	
40	At Matthew's house	9:9-13	2:13-17	5:27-32	
41	Questions about fasting	9:14-17	2:18-22	5:33-39	
42	Lame man at pool				5:1-18
43	Jesus claims: God's Son				5:19-30
44	Jesus supports His claim				5:31-47
45	Wheat gathering on Sabbath	12:1-8	2:23-28	6:1-5	
46	Jesus heals man's hand	12:9-14	3:1-6	6:6-11	
47	Crowds follow Jesus	12:15-21	3:7-12		
48	Jesus selects 12 disciples		3:13-19	6:12-16	
49	The Beatitudes	5:1-12		6:17-26	
50	Teaching of salt and light	5:13-16			
51	Teaching about the Law	5:17-20			
52	Teaching about anger	5:21-26			
53	Teaching about lust	5:27-30			
54	Teaching about divorce	5:31-32			
55	Teaching about vows	5:33-37			
56	Teaching about retaliation	5:38-42			
57	Teaching of loving enemies	5:43-48		6:27-36	
58	Teaching of giving to needy	6:1-4			
59	Teaching about prayer	6:5-15			
60	Teaching about fasting	6:16-18			
61	Teaching about money	6:19-24			
62	Teaching about worry	6:25-34			
63	Teaching of criticizing	7:1-6		6:37-42	
64	Ask, Seek, Knock	7:7-12			
65	Teaching of way to heaven	7:13-14			
66	Teaching of fruit in lives	7:15-20		6:43-45	

67	Houses on rock or sand	7:21-29		6:46-49	
68	Roman centurion's faith	8:5-13		7:1-10	
69	Widow's son raised			7:11-17	
70	John's doubt eased	11:1-19		7:18-35	
71	Rest for the soul	11:20-30			
72	Anointing feet of Jesus			7:36-50	
73	Women helpers			8:1-3	
74	Jesus accused	12:22-37	3:20-30		
75	Asking for a miracle	12:38-45			
76	True family described	12:46-50	3:31-35	8:19-21	
77	Parable of soils	13:1-9	4:1-9	8:4-8	
78	Explanations	13:10-23	4:10-25	8:9-18	
79	Parable of growing seed		4:26-29		
80	Parable of weeds	13:24-30			
81	Parable of mustard seed	13-31-32	4:30-34		
82	Parable of yeast	13:33-35			
83	Explaining weed parables	13:36-43			
84	Parable of hidden treasure	13:44			
85	Parable of pearl merchant	13:45-46			
86	Parable of the fishing net	13:47-52			
87	Jesus calms the storm	8:23-27	4:35-41	8:22-25	
88	Demons to herd of pigs	8:28-34	5:1-20	8:26-39	
89	Woman's issue; Jairus' girl	9:18-26	5:21-43	8:40-56	
90	Jesus heals blind, mute	9:27-34			
91	Nazareth refuses to believe	13:53-58	6:1-6		
92	Pray for workers	9:35-38			
93	Disciples sent out	10:1-16	6:7-13	9:1-6	
94	Preparation for persecution	10:17-42			
95	John the Baptist martyred	14:1-12	6:14-29	9:7-9	
96	5000 fed	14:13-21	6:30-44	9:10-17	6:1-15
97	Jesus walks on water	14:22-33	6:45-52		6:16-21
98	Healing those who touch	14:34-36	6:53-56		
99	Jesus: true Bread				6:22-40
100	Jews disagree				6:41-59
101	Many disciples desert				6:60-71
102	Teaching of inner purity	15:1-20	7:1-23		
103	Demon cast out of girl	15:21-28	7:24-30		
104	Crowd marvels at healings	15:29-31	7:31-37		
105	4000 fed	15:32-39	8:1-10		
106	Leaders ask for a sign	16:1-4	8:11-13		

107	Warning of wrong teaching	16:5-12	8:14-21		
108	Blind man healed		8:22-26		
109	Peter says Jesus is Messiah	16:13-20	8:27-30	9:18-20	
110	Jesus predicts His death	16:21-28	8:31-9:1	9:21-27	
111	Transfiguration	17:1-13	9:2-13	9:28-36	
112	Demon possessed healed	17:14-21	9:14-29	9:37-43	
113	Jesus predicts death again	17:22-23	9:30-32	9:44-45	
114	Coin in mouth of fish	17:24-27			
115	Argument about the greatest	18:1-6	9:33-37	9:46-48	
116	Disciples forbid another		9:38-41	9:49-50	
117	Warning about temptation	18:7-9	9:42-50		
118	Warning of prejudice	18:10-14			
119	Treatment sinning believer	18:15-20			
120	Parable unforgiving debtor	18:21-35			
121	Jesus' brothers ridicule Him				7:1-9
122	Cost of following Jesus	8:18-22		9:51-62	
123	Jesus teaches at temple				7:10-31
124	Leaders attempt to arrest				7:32-53
125	Jesus forgives adulteress				8:1-11
126	Jesus is Light of the world				8:12-20
127	Warning coming judgment				8:21-30
128	God's true children				8:31-47
129	Jesus states He is eternal				8:48-59
130	Jesus sends 72 messengers			10:1-16	
131	72 messengers return			10:17-24	
132	Parable of good Samaritan			10:25-37	
133	Visit to Mary and Martha			10:38-42	
134	Jesus teaches of prayer	6:9-13		11:1-13	
135	Jesus answers accusations			11:14-28	
136	Warning against unbelief			11:29-32	
137	Teaching of light within			11:33-36	
138	Jesus criticizes leaders			11:37-54	
139	Speaking against hypocrisy			12:1-12	
140	Parable of the rich fool			12:13-21	
141	Jesus warns about worry			12:22-34	
142	Prepare for His coming			12:35-48	
143	Warning of coming division			12:49-53	
144	Warning of future crisis			12:54-59	
145	Jesus calls for repentance			13:1-9	
146	Jesus heals crippled woman			13:10-17	

147	Teaching kingdom of God			13:18-21	
148	Jesus heals man born blind				9:1-12
149	Leaders question blind man				9:13-34
150	Teaching spiritual blindness				9:35-41
151	Jesus is the good Shepherd				10:1-21
152	Leaders surround Jesus				10:22-42
153	Teaching entering kingdom			13:22-30	
154	Jesus grieves over Jerusalem			13:31-35	
155	Healing of man with dropsy			14:1-6	
156	Teaching of seeking honor			14:7-14	
157	Parable of the great feast			14:15-24	
158	Cost of discipleship			14:25-35	
159	Parable of the lost sheep			15:1-7	
160	Parable of the lost coin			15:8-10	
161	Parable of the prodigal son			15:11-32	
162	Parable of shrewd manager			16:1-18	
163	Story rich man and beggar			16:19-31	
164	Forgiveness and faith			17:1-10	
165	Lazarus illness and death				11:1-16
166	Jesus with Mary, Martha				11:17-37
167	Jesus raises Lazarus				11:38-44
168	Leaders plot to kill Jesus				11:45-57
169	Jesus heals 10 lepers			17:11-19	
170	Teaching coming kingdom			17:20-37	
171	Parable of persistent widow			18:1-8	
172	Parable 2 men who prayed			18:9-14	
173	Teaching marriage, divorce	19:1-12	10:1-12		
174	Jesus blesses little children	19:13-15	10:13-16	18:15-17	
175	Jesus and rich young man	19:16-30	10:17-31	18:18-30	
176	Parable of equal pay	20:1-16			
177	Jesus predicts death 3rd time	20:17-19	10:32-34	18:31-34	
178	Jesus teaches serving others	20:20-28	10:35-45		
179	Jesus heals blind beggar	20:29-34	10:46-52	18:35-43	
180	Zacchaeus			19:1-10	
181	Parable of 10 servants			19:11-27	
182	Woman anoints perfume	26:6-13	14:3-9		12:1-11
183	Jesus rides into Jerusalem	21:1-11	11:1-11	19:28-44	12:12-19
184	Jesus clears temple again	21:12-17	11:12-19	19:45-48	
185	Jesus says why He must die				12:20-36
186	Most do not believe Jesus				12:37-43

187	Jesus summarizes message				12:44-50
188	Disciples can pray anything	21:18-22	11:20-26		
189	Leaders challenge authority	21:23-27	11:27-33	20:1-8	
190	Parable of 2 sons	21:28-32			
191	Parable of wicked tenants	21:33-46	12:1-12	20:9-19	
192	Parable of wedding feast	22:1-14			
193	Questions about taxes	22:15-22	12:13-17	20:20-26	
194	Questions: resurrection	22:23-33	12:18-27	20:27-40	
195	Questions of commandment	22:34-40	12:28-34		
196	Leaders have no answer	22:41-46	12:35-37	20:41-44	
197	Warning against leaders	23:1-12	12:38-40	20:45-47	
198	Leaders condemned	23:13-36			
199	Jesus grieves over Jerusalem	23:37-39			
200	Poor widow gives all		12:41-44	21:1-4	
201	Jesus tells about future	24:1-25	13:1-23	21:5-24	
202	Jesus tells about His return	24:26-35	13:24-31	21:25-33	
203	Remain watchful	24:36-51	13:32-37	21:34-38	
204	Parable of 10 bridesmaids	25:1-13			
205	Parable of loaned money	25:14-30			
206	Jesus tells of final judgment	25:31-46			
207	Leaders plot to kill Jesus	26:1-5	14:1-2	22:1-2	
208	Judas agrees to betray Jesus	26:14-16	14:10-11	22:3-6	
209	Disciples prepare Passover	26:17-19	14:12-16	22:7-13	
210	Jesus washes disciples' feet				13:1-20
211	The last supper	26:20-30	14:17-26	22:14-30	13:21-30
212	Peter's denial predicted			22:31-38	13:31-38
213	Jesus is way to the Father				14:1-14
214	Jesus promises Holy Spirit				14:15-31
215	The Vine and the branches				15:1-17
216	Warning of world's hatred				15:18-16:4
217	Jesus teaches of Holy Spirit				16:5-15
218	Using Jesus' name in prayer				16:16-33
219	Jesus prays for Himself				17:1-5
220	Jesus prays for His disciples				17:6-19
221	Prayer for future believers				17:20-26
222	Peter's denial predicted	26:31-35	14:27-31		
223	Jesus agonizes in garden	26:36-46	14:32-42	22:39-46	
224	Jesus betrayed and arrested	26:47-56	14:43-52	22:47-53	18:1-11
225	Annas questions Jesus				18:12-23
226	Caiaphas questions Jesus	26:57-68	14:53-65		

227	Peter denies Jesus	26:69-75	14:66-72	22:54-65	18:25-27
228	Leaders condemn Jesus	27:1-2	15:1	22:66-71	
229	Judas kills himself	27:3-10			
230	Jesus on trial before Pilate	27:11-14	15:2-5	23:1-5	18:28-37
231	Jesus on trial before Herod			23:6-12	
232	Pilate releases Jesus: crucify	27:15-26	15:6-15	23:13-25	18:38-19:16
233	Roman soldiers mock Jesus	27:27-31	15:16-20		
234	Jesus led away: crucifixion	27:32-34	15:21-24	23:26-31	19:17
235	Jesus placed on the cross	27:35-44	15:25-32	23:32-43	19:18-27
236	Jesus dies on the cross	27:45-56	15:33-41	23:44-49	19:28-37
237	Jesus laid in tomb	27:57-61	15:42-47	23:50-56	19:38-42
238	Guards posted at the tomb	27:62-66			
239	Jesus rises from the dead	28:1-7	16:1-8	24:1-12	20:1-9
240	Jesus appears to Mary Mag.		16:9-11		20:10-18
241	Jesus appears to the women	28:8-10			
242	Leaders bribe the guards	28:11-15			
243	Travelers on Emmaus Road		16:12-13	24:13-35	
244	Jesus appears to disciples			24:36-43	20:19-23
245	Jesus appears to Thomas		16:14		20:24-31
246	Jesus and disciples fishing				21:1-14
247	Jesus talks with Peter				21:15-25
248	Jesus gives commission	28:16-20	16:15-18		
249	Jesus, disciples in Jerusalem			24:44-49	
250	Jesus ascends to Heaven		16:19-20	24:50-53	

NIV Chronology

Compiled and charted by Jane Weathers

BIBLIOGRAPHY

Abbott, Steve. Sermons at First Baptist Church, Siloam Springs, Arkansas.

Anderson, Carl R. "Ezra, Esther, Nehemiah." *HCSB Study Bible: Holman Christian Standard Study Bible: God's Word for Life*. Nashville, TN: Holman Bible Publishers, 2010.

Barabas, S., contrib. *The Zondervan Pictorial Encyclopedia of the Bible in Five Volumes*. Ed. Tenney, Merrill C. Grand Rapids, MI. The Zondervan Corporation, 1975.

Beyer, Bryan E. "1 and 2 Samuel." *HCSB Study Bible: Holman Christian Standard Study Bible: God's Word for Life*. Nashville, TN: Holman Bible Publishers, 2010.

Biography.com. A&E Television Networks, LLC.

Blum, Edwin A. "Romans." *HCSB Study Bible: Holman Christian Standard Study Bible: God's Word for Life*. Nashville, TN: Holman Bible Publishers, 2010.

Bowling, Andrew C. "1 and 2 Kings." *HCSB Study Bible: Holman Christian Standard Study Bible: God's Word for Life*. Nashville, TN: Holman Bible Publishers, 2010.

Britannica.com. Encyclopaedia Britannica. Inc.

Clendenen, E. Ray. "Hosea, Malachi, Matthew." *HCSB Study Bible: Holman Christian Standard Study Bible: God's Word for Life*. Nashville, TN: Holman Bible Publishers, 2010.

Coker, W. B., contrib. *The Zondervan Pictorial Encyclopedia of the Bible in Five Volumes*. Ed. Tenney, Merrill C. Grand Rapids, MI. The Zondervan Corporation, 1975.

Cole, R. Dennis. "Numbers." *HCSB Study Bible: Holman Christian Standard Study Bible: God's Word for Life*. Nashville, TN: Holman Bible Publishers, 2010.

Coover-Cox, Dorian G. "Exodus." *HCSB Study Bible: Holman Christian Standard Study Bible: God's Word for Life*. Nashville, TN: Holman Bible Publishers, 2010.

Corduan, Winfried. "1 and 2 Chronicles." *HCSB Study Bible: Holman Christian Standard Study Bible: God's Word for Life*. Nashville, TN: Holman Bible Publishers, 2010.

Darmani, Lawrence, contrib. *Our Daily Bread*. Eds. Cetas, Anne, et al. Grand Rapids, MI: Our Daily Bread Ministries, (n.d.).

Davis, James F. "Thessalonians." *HCSB Study Bible: Holman Christian Standard Study Bible: God's Word for Life*. Nashville, TN: Holman Bible Publishers, 2010.

Davis, John J. *Moses and the Gods of Egypt*. Winona Lake, IN: BMH Books and Baker Book House, 1971.

Dockery, David S. "Ephesians." *HCSB Study Bible: Holman Christian Standard Study Bible: God's Word for Life*. Nashville, TN: Holman Bible Publishers, 2010.

Duguid, Iain M. "Judges." *HCSB Study Bible: Holman Christian Standard Study Bible: God's Word for Life*. Nashville, TN: Holman Bible Publishers, 2010.

Easley, Kendell H. "Second Corinthians." *HCSB Study Bible: Holman Christian Standard Study Bible: God's Word for Life*. Nashville, TN: Holman Bible Publishers, 2010.

Ellicott, Charles John, ed. *Ellicott's Commentary of the Whole Bible, Vol. II-V.* Grand Rapids, MI: Zondervan Publishing House, 1954.

ESV: *The Holy Bible: English Standard Version.* Wheaton, IL: Crossway Bibles, Good News Publishers, 2004.

Feinberg, C. L., contrib. *The Zondervan Pictorial Encyclopedia of the Bible in Five Volumes.* Ed. Tenney, Merrill C. Grand Rapids, MI. The Zondervan Corporation, 1975.

Fisher, Dennis, contrib. *Our Daily Bread.* Eds. Cetas, Anne, et al. Grand Rapids, MI: Our Daily Bread Ministries, 16 Sept. 2016.

Garrett, Duane A. "Amos, Ecclesiastes." *HCSB Study Bible: Holman Christian Standard Study Bible: God's Word for Life.* Nashville, TN: Holman Bible Publishers, 2010.

Graham, Franklin. Speech, Billy Graham Evangelistic Association, Charlotte, NC.

Halley, Henry H. *Halley's Bible Handbook; An Abbreviated Bible Commentary. Grand* Rapids, MI: Zondervan Publishing House, 1959.

Hamilton, F. E., *contrib. The Zondervan Pictorial Encyclopedia of the Bible in Five Volumes.* Ed. Tenney, Merrill C. Grand Rapids, MI. The Zondervan Corporation, 1975.

Harris, Murray J. "Philemon." *HCSB Study Bible: Holman Christian Standard Study Bible: God's Word for Life.* Nashville, TN: Holman Bible Publishers, 2010.

HCSB Study Bible: Holman Christian Standard Study Bible: God's Word for Life. Nashville, TN: Holman Bible Publishers, 2010.

Healthgrades.com. Healthgrades Operating Company, Inc.

Hess, Richard S. "Joshua." *HCSB Study Bible: Holman Christian Standard Study Bible: God's Word for Life.* Nashville, TN: Holman Bible Publishers, 2010.

History.com. A&E Television Networks, LLC.

Holdcroft, L. Thomas. *The Pentateuch.* Oakland, CA: Western Book Company, 1966.

Institute for Creation Research, icr.org

Jeremiah, David. Lecture on Turning Point broadcast, San Diego, CA.

Jones, Timothy Paul. "Bible Time Line." Torrance, CA: Rose Publishing, 2005.

Kaiser, Walter C. "Jeremiah." *HCSB Study Bible: Holman Christian Standard Study Bible: God's Word for Life.* Nashville, TN: Holman Bible Publishers, 2010.

KJV: *The Scofield Reference Bible: Authorized King James Version.* New York: Oxford University Press, 1945

Kostenberger, Andreas J. "John, Colossians." *HCSB Study Bible: Holman Christian Standard Study Bible: God's Word for Life.* Nashville, TN: Holman Bible Publishers, 2010.

Linzey, Gene. "Bible Answers: Finding a spot between hot, cold." *Siloam Springs* (AR) *Herald Leader,* 2008.

Linzey, S. Eugene. *Reflectionss on Faith and History: Bringing Scripture to Life.* Middletown DE: 2018. 130.

Livingston, G. H., contrib. *The Zondervan Pictorial Encyclopedia of the Bible in Five Volumes.* Ed. Tenney, Merrill C. Grand Rapids, MI. The Zondervan Corporation, 1975.

Longman III, Tremper. "Isaiah." *HCSB Study Bible: Holman Christian Standard Study Bible: God's Word for Life*. Nashville, TN: Holman Bible Publishers, 2010.

Luter, A. Boyd. "Luke, Galatians, Revelation." *HCSB Study Bible: Holman Christian Standard Study Bible: God's Word for Life*. Nashville, TN: Holman Bible Publishers, 2010.

MacArthur, John. Lecture on Grace to You broadcast, Panorama City, CA.

Macfarlan, Laura. "Choosing Faith Over Fear," "True Friendship." Siloam Springs, AR: CrossMyHeartMinistry.com.

Mathews, Kenneth A. "Leviticus." *HCSB Study Bible: Holman Christian Standard Study Bible: God's Word for Life*. Nashville, TN: Holman Bible Publishers, 2010.

McGee, J. Vernon. Lectures on Thru the Bible broadcast, Pasadena, CA.

McLaren, Ross H. "Mark." *HCSB Study Bible: Holman Christian Standard Study Bible: God's Word for Life*. Nashville, TN: Holman Bible Publishers, 2010.

Melick, Jr., Richard R. "Philippians." *HCSB Study Bible: Holman Christian Standard Study Bible: God's Word for Life*. Nashville, TN: Holman Bible Publishers, 2010.

Merrill, Eugene H. "Deuteronomy." *HCSB Study Bible: Holman Christian Standard Study Bible: God's Word for Life*. Nashville, TN: Holman Bible Publishers, 2010.

Mazar, Benjamin, ed. *The World of the Bible, Vol. 1-5*. New York, Philadelphia, Chicago, Los Angeles, San Francisco: Educational Heritage, Inc., / Yonkers, 1959.

Metzger, Bruce M. and Coogan, Michael D., eds. *The Oxford Companion to the Bible*. New York: Oxford University Press, 1993.

Moorehead, W. G. *Outline Studies in the Old Testament.* Grand Rapids, MI: Zondervan, reprinted from the Fleming H. Revel Co. edition, 1893.

Myers, Jeremy, redeeminggod.com.

NIV: *Life Application Bible: New International Version.* Wheaton IL, Grand Rapids, MI: Tyndale House Publishers and Zondervan Publishing House, 1991.

Ochoa, Keila, contrib. *Our Daily Bread.* Eds. Cetas, Anne, et al. Grand Rapids, MI: Our Daily Bread Ministries, 16 Sept. 2016.

Payne, J. B., contrib. *The Zondervan Pictorial Encyclopedia of the Bible in Five Volumes.* Ed. Tenney, Merrill C. Grand Rapids, MI. The Zondervan Corporation, 1975.

Platt, David. *A Global Gospel in a World of Religions,* Radical, 2016.

Porter, Stanley E. "Acts." *HCSB Study Bible: Holman Christian Standard Study Bible: God's Word for Life.* Nashville, TN: Holman Bible Publishers, 2010.

Quarles, Charles L. "Matthew." *HCSB Study Bible: Holman Christian Standard Study Bible: God's Word for Life.* Nashville, TN: Holman Bible Publishers, 2010.

Register, Dean. *Explore the Bible: Acts.* Nashville, TN: LifeWay Christian Resources, 2016.

Rogers, Adrian. Lecture on Love Worth Finding broadcast, Memphis, TN

Rooker, Mark F. "Ezekiel." *HCSB Study Bible: Holman Christian Standard Study Bible: God's Word for Life.* Nashville, TN: Holman Bible Publishers, 2010.

Rydelnick, Michael. "Daniel." *HCSB Study Bible: Holman Christian Standard Study Bible: God's Word for Life.* Nashville, TN: Holman Bible Publishers, 2010.

Sandy, D. Brent. "Zechariah." *HCSB Study Bible: Holman Christian Standard Study Bible: God's Word for Life.* Nashville, TN: Holman Bible Publishers, 2010.

Smith, Arthur E. *Studies in Leviticus with illustrations*, reprinted St. Louis, MO: Bible Memory Association, 1976.

Sprinkle, Joe. "Jonah, Habakkuk." *HCSB Study Bible: Holman Christian Standard Study Bible: God's Word for Life.* Nashville, TN: Holman Bible Publishers, 2010.

Tenney, Merrill C., ed., *The Zondervan Pictorial Encyclopedia of the Bible in Five Volumes.* Grand Rapids, MI. The Zondervan Corporation, 1975.

Tilley, Allen. *Explore the Bible: Numbers and Deuteronomy.* Nashville, TN: LifeWay Christian Resources, 2019

Tomlinson, F. Alan. "First Corinthians." *HCSB Study Bible: Holman Christian Standard Study Bible: God's Word for Life.* Nashville, TN: Holman Bible Publishers, 2010.

Van Neste, Ray. "Timothy, Titus." *HCSB Study Bible: Holman Christian Standard Study Bible: God's Word for Life.* Nashville, TN: Holman Bible Publishers, 2010.

Waltke, B. K., contrib. *The Zondervan Pictorial Encyclopedia of the Bible in Five Volumes.* Ed. Tenney, Merrill C. Grand Rapids, MI. The Zondervan Corporation, 1975.

Walvoord, John F. *Daniel: The Key to Prophetic Revelation.* Chicago: Moody Press, 1971.

Weathers, Ted. "Daniel – a Quick Overview." Unpublished article. Siloam Springs, AR, 2010.

White, Jr., W., contrib. *The Zondervan Pictorial Encyclopedia of the Bible in Five Volumes.* Ed. Tenney, Merrill C. Grand Rapids, MI. The Zondervan Corporation, 1975.

Wilder Terry L. "Peter, Jude." *HCSB Study Bible: Holman Christian Standard Study Bible: God's Word for Life.* Nashville, TN: Holman Bible Publishers, 2010.

Wikipedia.org. Wikimedia Foundation.

Yarbrough, Robert W. "1, 2, 3 John." *HCSB Study Bible: Holman Christian Standard Study Bible: God's Word for Life.* Nashville, TN: Holman Bible Publishers, 2010.

Yarnell III, Malcolm B. "Hebrews." *HCSB Study Bible: Holman Christian Standard Study Bible: God's Word for Life.* Nashville, TN: Holman Bible Publishers, 2010

ENDORSEMENTS

Why do some events appear to have been completed, but several chapters later – or in another book of the Bible – the same thing is told as though it had not yet happened. Why do we read that some Biblical events happened prior to their historical timeframe?

Except for the Pentateuch, the books of the Bible were not necessarily written sequentially. Even chapters within the books are not necessarily sequential.

That's why when I read Jane Becker Weathers' chronological reading guide, I was impressed. As a historian, I believe it's beneficial to understand Holy Scripture in its proper historical setting, and in light of world events. Jane Weathers' reading guide is invaluable in this respect.

Chronological Bible Reading Guide – God's Word, The Word of Light and Life not only lists a weekly-daily reading plan, it also presents historical data relating to that point of Biblical history. In my estimation, that is what sets this guide apart from all others.

Jane doesn't break the chronology down verse-by-verse (which is very tedious and delicate), but she does present a sequential chapter-by-chapter plan, and I highly endorse this Biblical/historical chronological reading guide. Keep it with your Bible as you read.

S. Eugene Linzey
Former Pastor
Author of *Charter of the Christian Faith*

The *Chronological Bible Reading Guide* by Jane Becker Weathers is a wonderful tool for personal Bible study. The additional insights gleaned from various Bible scholars add depth and meaning to a chronological reading of the scriptures, and enhance the discovery of innumerable treasures in God's Word. Theologian John Stott said, "We must allow the Word of God to confront us, to disturb us, to undermine our complacency and to overthrow our patterns of thought and behavior." With this in mind, Hebrews 4:12 takes on even greater significance, "For the word of God is quick, and powerful, and sharper than any two edged sword..." My prayer is that by following this Bible reading guide, you will find that God's word provides "a lamp to your feet and a light for your path." (Psalm 119:105)

John G Gage
Former worship pastor-retired
Author: *Love, Dad; Character For Kids; Encouragement in Adversity*
www.johnggage.com

Jane Weathers' goal in producing this study tool was to arrange the chapters of the Bible into chronologically ordered groups so that each chapter can serve as *"supplementary background commentary"* for the other chapters that overlapped from the same general time period. For example, in this work, week 30, Day 2 (p. 70), groups together Isaiah 38, 2 Kings 20, Isaiah 39, and 2nd Chronicles 32. Thus, for these four chapters, the reader has immediately in hand four chapters that overlap temporally. Each of the four, then, might serve as immediate Biblical commentary on the other three. A fuller treatment of Hezekiah's illness and recovery and his foolish display of wealth is enhanced by dealing with all four chapters.

Further, since the temporal boundaries of the different days readings do not exactly coincide, chapters from both preceding and following days might also provide some *commentary* value for the readings of any particular day. Thus, Weathers' study provides a reading guide for using the Bible as its own commentary. I judge that Mrs. Weathers has achieved her goal.

However, the writer does more. She also provides occasional extra observations and comments from other outside studies and personal observations. This material is wisely limited, because if it were too extensive, it would distract attention from her major goal, i.e. to let the Bible speak for itself on these topics. I judge that she has used just enough extra biblical comment to accomplish two good goals. First, to demonstrate her own good judgment in what she selected for additional interesting comment. And, second, at the same time, to vary the routine of comparing passages on the same topic with reasonably limited general comments that bring other ideas into the discussion.

Andrew C. Bowling
Retired Bible Professor and interim Pastor supply
Co-author of *Understanding Biblical Hebrew Verb Forms: Distribution and Function across Genres*
Author of "1-2 Chronicles": in *Evangelical Commentary on the Bible*

ABOUT THE AUTHOR

Jane Weathers grew up on a small farm in South Dakota, the youngest of six children. She received a B.S. degree in education from John Brown University, and taught for twenty-four years, mostly in Christian schools. She taught students of all ages during those years, and worked one-on-one with children with learning difficulties. A highlight was teaching Bible lessons and stories with applications to little ones starting their learning years in kindergarten.

Jane's passion for the Bible, led her to study what Bible scholars had to say about various scriptures. During a fifteen-year period she arranged her own time line for the text, and developed her *Chronological Bible Reading Guide*.

Jane and her husband, Ted, reside in Siloam Springs, Arkansas. They have three married sons and six grandchildren.

More information can be found at www.ChronoBibleGuide.com.

Printed in the United States
By Bookmasters